General editor: Graha

Brodie's Notes on Chaucer's

The Franklin's Tale

F. W. Robinson MA

MACMILLAN

First published 1986 by James Brodie Ltd
This edition first published 1978
by Pan Books Ltd

Reprinted 1992 by
THE MACMILLAN PRESS LTD
Houndmills, Basingstoke, Hampshire RG21 2XS
and London
Companies and representatives
throughout the world

ISBN 0-333-58062-1

Printed in Great Britain by
Mackays of Chatham PLC
Chatham, Kent

11 10   9   8   7   6   5   4   3
06 05 04 03 02 01 00 99 98

Contents

Editor's note and bibliography

Chaucer is our greatest comic poet, and *The Canterbury Tales* is his masterpiece. Yet Chaucer's poetry is not a subject for general reading, but of specialist study. The reason for this is that his language is not easy for the general reader to read and understand. The English language of the fourteenth century was different from the language we speak today, and some trouble must be taken in learning these differences before a proper understanding of the meaning can be gained. And further, when one has learned to read Chaucer and to understand the meaning, some knowledge is necessary of the age in which he lived, and his place in it, before the work of this colourful and humorous poet can be fully appreciated and enjoyed.

These notes are aimed primarily at students coming fresh to Chaucer in their studies of English literature. An attempt has been made to set out, as briefly and simply as possible, the areas of knowledge which are necessary for the proper understanding and appreciation of a selected text in the context of examination requirements at Ordinary and Advanced Levels. It is hoped, however, that the notes have been prepared in such a way that the student will enjoy the task of understanding and appreciating this wonderful poetry with its melodic style, gentle satire and rollicking humour, and even to acquire a taste for Chaucer which will lead to wider reading and a deeper appreciation of his work.

The Editor wishes to acknowledge his indebtedness to the various works he has studied, and particularly to the editions of Chaucer's works by Professors W. W. Skeat and F. N. Robinson (it is on the latter's work that the text of this edition is based – *The Complete Works of Geoffrey Chaucer*, 2nd ed., 1957, with revised punctuation and spelling by James

Winny. CUP 1971). There are also editions of several of Chaucer's *Tales* edited by F. W. Robinson and published by James Brodie Ltd.

Bibliography

For those who wish to carry their study of Chaucer beyond what is possible to include in a small volume of notes, a selection of books that may be helpful is listed below:

The Poet Chaucer Nevill Coghill, OUP Paperbacks
An Introduction to Chaucer Hussey, CUP
English Social History Trevelyan (Chaps 1 and 2) Longmans, also Penguin
Chaucer's World M. Hussey, CUP
Pelican Guide to English Literature ed. B. Ford, Vol. 1, The Age of Chaucer, Penguin Books

It is recommended that students should read a selection of the tales from the translation into modern verse by Nevill Coghill – *The Canterbury Tales*, translated by Nevill Coghill, Penguin Classics.

It is also recommended that students should listen to a recording of Chaucer read with the original pronunciation: *The Prologue to The Canterbury Tales*, read in Middle English by Nevill Coghill, Norman Davis and John Burrow. Argo Record Company, London, No. PLP 1001 (LP).

A brief description of
Chaucer's life and works

Geoffrey Chaucer was born about 1340 near the Tower of
London. He was born into the age of Edward III, and of
the Black Prince, into the Age of Chivalry and the magnifi-
cent court of Edward III with knights and ladies, heraldry
and tournaments, minstrels and poetry, music and storytelling.
   Chaucer entered into this rich and colourful courtly world
at an early age when he became a page in the household of
the Countess of Ulster, wife to Lionel, later Duke of Clarence,
and one of the sons of Edward III. This was clearly arranged
by his parents, who had some contacts at Court. His mother's
first husband had been Keeper of the King's Wardrobe, and
there can be little doubt that she had something to do with
the appointment of Chaucer's father as deputy to the King's
Butler. The first record of Geoffrey Chaucer appears in an
account book, dating from 1357, which records a payment
by the royal household to a London tailor for a cloak, multi-
coloured breeches and a pair of shoes for the young page
Chaucer. It was in the Duke's great houses in London and
Yorkshire that the young page would have learned the elegant
and aristocratic code of manners, and made the acquaintance
of the high and the noble. He would have learned French
and Latin, the languages of the Court, the Church and the
educated classes. It was also one of the duties of a page to
play and sing, and to recite poetry.
   The next record we have is that Chaucer was taken prisoner
by the French in 1359, during one of the campaigns in the
Hundred Years' War, and ransomed in the following year –
the King himself contributing £16 (a very large sum in those
days) of the money. So Chaucer must have seen active service
in the French wars, probably as a squire attending on one
of the nobles, like the squire in the *Canterbury Tales* who

attended on the Knight, his father. For the upper classes, the experience of being a prisoner of war in the Age of Chivalry was not too uncomfortable. It was normal for the 'prisoner' to be entertained as a 'house guest' until the ransom was paid, and it is probable that during this enforced stay in France Chaucer became thoroughly versed in French literature, particularly the '*Roman de la Rose*' (the procedure manual, as it were, for 'courtly love'), which was to have such an important influence on his literary work.

After his ransom was paid, Chaucer returned to his Court duties, and was soon in a more elevated position. He became one of the valets in attendance on the King. In 1366 his father died and his mother married again. It is probable that in the same year he married Philippa, daughter of Sir Payne Roet and sister of Katherine Swynford, the mistress and later third wife to John of Gaunt. Philippa was a lady-in-waiting to the Queen. As a valet to the King, Chaucer would carry candles 'before the King', tidy up his bedroom and attend to a variety of duties which were to become more and more concerned with affairs of state. In 1368 he was sent abroad on the official business of the Crown. About this time he was promoted from valet to palace official. It appears that Chaucer went soldiering again in 1369, probably on one of John of Gaunt's campaigns in Picardy. In 1370 he was abroad again on the King's service, and we can now see him becoming a trusted civil servant as he was frequently sent on missions to France, Flanders and Italy. During his visits to Italy on official business Chaucer took the opportunity to become familiar with Italian literature, most especially the works of Petrarch, Boccaccio and Dante, which were to influence much of his subsequent poetry.

In 1374 he was promoted to a senior position as Comptroller of Customs and Subsidy (for wool, skins and hides), at the Port of London, and the City of London bestowed on him the lease of a house in Aldgate.

From about 1380 Chaucer settled down to his life as senior customs official, as there is only one record of further journeys abroad. He must have been respected as a man of affairs, as he became a Justice of the Peace in 1385, and a Member of Parliament, or Knight of the Shire for Kent, soon afterwards.

It was during these years that Chaucer found time to write seriously. His early literary attempts were influenced considerably by French literature. Then, when John of Gaunt left the country in 1386 on an adventure to claim the crown of Castile, the King's uncle, the Duke of Gloucester, took charge of the country's affairs (Richard being not yet of age), and Chaucer suffered from the new influences in royal patronage. He lost his Comptrollership of Customs, he was not re-elected to Parliament and he had to give up his house in Aldgate. We even learn that he felt himself in danger of being sued for debt. Chaucer had now plenty of time to ponder and at this time he must have been preparing *The Canterbury Tales*.

In 1389 a rumour was abroad that the great Duke of Lancaster (Chaucer's patron John of Gaunt) was returning home. This helped the young King Richard II in taking over the reins of power from his uncle Gloucester. It has been stated that the young King Richard knew Chaucer and liked his poetry. There must be some substance in this, as shortly afterwards Chaucer was appointed Clerk of the King's Works. John of Gaunt returned to England in November 1389, and for the rest of his life Chaucer was to enjoy royal patronage and a comfortable living. It was in these years of semi-retirement that *The Canterbury Tales* were written. Alas, Chaucer died without having finished his masterpiece. His tomb in Westminster Abbey gives the date of his death – October 1400.

It seems probable that 1387 was the approximate date of commencement for *The Canterbury Tales*. Chaucer's renown rests mainly on this work, but in terms of volume the *Tales*

form less than half of his writing which has come down to
us. Besides a number of shorter poems, there are five other
major works in verse and two or three in prose. Chaucer's
most important production during his first tentative years as
a writer was the translation he probably made of the *Roman
de la Rose*, the style and content of which were to have such
a great influence on his writing. His first major poem was
The Book of the Duchess, a poem steeped in the French tradi-
tion, written about 1370 to commemorate the death of
Blanche, Duchess of Lancaster and wife of his patron, John
of Gaunt. This was the first of four love-vision poems, the
others being *The House of Fame*, *The Parliament of Fowls* and
The Legend of Good Women (whose date is doubtful). Chaucer's
works can be conveniently grouped into three parts, the
French period, the Italian period and the English period;
and, generally speaking, the periods follow one another in
chronological sequence. The French period showed influence
of the *Roman de la Rose*, and included the love-vision poems.
The Italian period (1380–5) is marked by the narrative
poem *Troilus and Criseyde*, rehandles a theme of the Italian
poet Boccaccio. *Troilus and Criseyde* is a masterpiece, and is
still considered to be the finest narrative poem in English,
full of beauty and lyrical quality, and delightful humour in
the character of Pandarus. The English period (1389–1400)
is the last, and is the period when Chaucer reached his
full maturity as a dramatic poet. This is the period of *The
Canterbury Tales*, a collection of tales and tellers that is unique
in English literature. Chaucer died before he could complete
this great masterpiece.

It must be emphasized that these terms, 'French,' 'Italian',
'English' for Chaucer's literary life only indicate predominant
influences: the stories in *The Canterbury Tales* are drawn from
far and wide; *The Knight's Tale*, for instance, again owes its
theme to a story by Boccaccio.

The setting of the *Tale*

In his 'Prologue' to *The Canterbury Tales* Chaucer tells us
that he had already taken up his quarters at the Tabard
Inn, Southwark, preparatory to beginning, next day, his pilgrimage to Canterbury Cathedral – when twenty-nine others
appeared at the Inn, intent on the same purpose. These new-
comers had presumably met one another as they converged
upon London, and soon adopted the poet as a member of
their party. The host, Harry Bailly, realizing that this company was the pleasantest he had seen in the tavern that year,
proposed that they should while away the tedium of the
journey of four days by telling one another stories, suggesting
that each should tell two on the outward and two on the
homeward way. The proposal was adopted without dissent;
and as the host announced his intention of travelling with
his guests, they appointed him judge of the tales and
general referee. They approved his plan that, on their return,
the teller of the best tale should be entertained to supper,
at the Tabard, at the others' expense. The company then
retired to bed, and commenced the journey early next morning. A mile or so along the Kent Road the host pulled up by a
brook, where it was decided by lot that the Knight, the
most distinguished of the party, should tell the first tale.

The day was apparently April the seventeenth. They had
been called by the Host at cockcrow; and before night over-
took them at Dartford they had heard tales from the Knight,
the Miller, the Reeve, and the Cook. They seem to have
overslept the next morning after their first day's travelling, for
they did not leave the inn until ten o'clock. They were
entertained on their way by the Man of Law, the Shipman,
the Prioress, the Monk, and the Nun's Priest, while Chaucer
himself had told them two stories: one in verse, 'Sir Thopas';

and one in prose. They slept that night at Rochester. On their third day they heard the Doctor, the Pardoner, the Wife of Bath, the Friar, and the Summoner, as well as the Clerk and the Merchant. It was not until the last day of their journey to Canterbury that the Host called on the Squire – the youngest of them all, and son of the Knight – to fulfil his promise. He had already begun by nine in the morning; for they had got up early as they were to reach their destination before nightfall.

His long-winded tale was never finished. He had introduced the King of Tartary – Cambinskan – his wife, their two sons and Canacee, their lovely daughter, as well as the Knight, who had come from the King 'of Arabie and of Inde', with a 'stede of bras' for the King and a 'mirour and this ring' for the Princess. The second part of the tale concerns magical happenings in which Canacee is involved, and ends with promises of more 'adventures and batailles' connected with suitors for her hand.

Part three begins with the words:

'Appollo whirleth up his char so hye,
Til that the god Mercurius hous the slye—'

and that was all that Chaucer wrote of it.

As though the Squire's Tale had been completed, Chaucer now introduced a commendation from the Franklin, who expressed his view that no one of the other pilgrims could rival him in eloquence, congratulated him on his powers of judgement, and praised his good manners.

The Host, apparently objecting to the compliment paid to the Squire, brusquely calls on the Franklin for his own tale without any more ado: with the hope that the tale he has to tell will not displease the Host, the Franklin readily obeys.

The Franklin's Tale in Chaucer's original
Middle English, with a translation into
Modern English

The aim here has been to render, as accurately as possible
in Modern English, the sense of Chaucer's Middle English.
It has, of course, been necessary at times – for clarity of
understanding – to depart from a literal translation of
Chaucer's words. On the other hand, the older forms of
sentence construction have, on a number of occasions, been
preserved where the sense is clear. We hope that our Study
Aid will serve to encourage the student, fairly soon in his
reading, to savour the tale in the beauty of its original.

*Here follows the account of the Franklin
from the general prologue* (lines 331 to 360)

A Frankeleyn was in his companye;
Whit was his berd as is the dayesye;
Of his complexioun he was sangwyn.
Wel loved he by the morwe a sop in wyn;
To liven in delyt was ever his wone,
For he was Epicurus owne sone,
That heeld opinioun that pleyn delyt
Was verraily felicitee parfyt.
An housholdere, and that a greet, was he;
Seint Julian he was in his contree;
His breed, his ale, was alwey after oon;
A bettre envyned man was nowher noon.
Withoute bakemete was never his hous,   340
Of fissh and flessh, and that so plentevous,
It snewed in his hous of mete and drinke,
Of alle deyntees that men coude thinke.

After the sondry sesons of the yeer,
So chaunged he his mete and his soper.
Ful many a fat partrich hadde he in mewe,
And many a breem and many a luce in stewe.   350
Wo was his cook but-if his sauce were
Poynaunt and sharp, and redy al his gere.
His table dormant in his halle alway
Stood redy covered al the longe day.

At sessiouns ther was he lord and sire;
Ful oftetyme he was knight of the shire.
An anlaas, and gipser al of silk,
Heeng at his girdel whit as morne milk.
A shirreve hadde he been and a countour;
Was nowher such a worthy vavasour.   360

Here follows the account of the Franklin from the General Prologue (lines 331–60)

In the company there was a Franklin, with a beard white as a daisy; ruddy in looks and sanguine of temperament. He dearly loved to take, each morning, a sop of bread in his wine. To live for pleasure was always his principle, for he was Epicurus's own son – he who held the view that complete enjoyment was truly the most perfect happiness. He was a householder, and a great one as well: a very Saint Julian in his part of the country. His bread and ale were always of the best; and no one anywhere had a better stock of wine. His house was never without pasties, of both fish and meat – and in such abundance that it was as if, in his house, it snowed food and drink and all the delicacies one could think of.

According to the season of the year he changed his meat and his menu. He kept many a fat partridge in his enclosure, and many a bream and pike in his pond. Woe betide the cook if his sauce were not piquant and sharp, and all his utensils prepared and ready for use. In his hall his solid table stood always ready, fully prepared all day long.

At court sessions he was lord and master; and very often he was knight of the shire in Parliament. At his girdle hung a dagger, and a silk purse, white as the morning milk. He had been a sheriff and an accountant, and nowhere was there such a worthy country gentleman.

Here folwen the wordes of the Frankelin to the
Squier, and the wordes of the Host to the Frankelin

'In feith, Squier, thou hast thee wel y-quit,
And gentilly I preise wel thy wit,'
Quod the Frankeleyn, 'considering thy youthe,
So feelingly thou spekest, sir, I allow the!
As to my doom, there is non that is here
Of eloquence that shal be thy pere,
If that thou live; god yeve thee good chaunce,
And in vertu sende thee continuaunce!
For of they speche I have greet deyntee.
I have a sone, and, by the Trinitee,   10
I hadde lever than twenty pound worth lond,
Though it right now were fallen in myn hond,
He were a man of swich discrecioun
As that ye been! fy on possessioun
But-if a man be vertuous with-al.
I have my sone snibbed, and yet shal,
For he to vertu listeth nat entende;
But for to pleye at dees, and to despende,
And lese al that he hath, is his usage,
And he hath lever talken with a page   20
Than to comune with any gentil wight
Ther he mighte lerne gentillesse aright.'

'Straw for your gentillesse,' quod our host;
'What, frankeleyn? pardee, sir, wel thou wost
That eche of yow mot tellen atte leste
A tale or two, or breken his biheste.'

'That knowe I wel, sir,' quod the frankeleyn;
'I prey yow, haveth me nat in desdeyn
Though to this man I speke a word or two.'

'Telle on thy tale, with-outen wordes mo.'   30
'Gladly, sir host,' quod he, 'I wol obeye
Un-to your wil; now herkneth what I seye.
I wol yow nat contrarien in no wyse
As fer as that my wittes wol suffyse;
I prey to god that it may plesen yow,
Than woot I wel that it is good y-now.'

Here follow the words of the Franklin to the Squire, and the words of the Host to the Franklin

'Truly, Squire, you have acquitted yourself well, and like a gentleman, and I give full praise to your intelligence,' the Franklin said. 'Considering your youth, you speak most feelingly, sir, and I must commend you. In my judgement, there is no one here who will equal you in eloquence as long as you live; God give you good fortune and grant you a long and successful future. I myself have a son and, by the Trinity, rather than have twenty pounds' worth of land – though it should fall straight into my hands – I would prefer that my son should become a man of such discretion as you are. A plague on possessions unless a man has accomplishments to go with them. I have chided my son, and will go on doing so, for he is not inclined to pay any attention: all he does is play at dice and squander his money, and lose everything that he has. And this is his manner of life: he would rather talk to a page than to a gentleman from whom he might truly learn something of good breeding.'

'A straw for your good breeding!' exclaimed our host, 'eh, Franklin! By God, sir, you know very well that each of you must tell at least a tale or two – or break his promise.'

'I know that well, sir,' replied the Franklin, 'I pray you, do not scorn me just because I speak a word or two to this man.'

'Go on with your tale, without more ado.'

'Gladly, sir host,' he said, 'I will submit to your will; now listen to what I have to say. I will do as you wish in every way, as far as I am able. I pray to God that it may please you; then I will know that it is good enough.'

The Prolog of the Frankeleyns Tale

   Thise olde gentil Britons in hir dayes
Of diverse aventures maden layes,
Rymeyed in hir firste Briton tonge;
Which layes with hir instruments they songe,   40
Or elles redden hem for hir plesaunce;
And oon of hem have I in remembraunce,
Which I shal seyn with good wil as I can.
   But, sires, by-cause I am a burel man,
At my biginning first I yow biseche
Have me excused of my rude speche;
I lerned never rethoryk certeyn;
Thing that I speke, it moot be bare and pleyn.
I sleep never on the mount of Pernaso,
Ne lerned Marcus Tullius Cithero.   50
Colours ne knowe I none, with-outen drede,
But swiche colours as growen in the mede,
Or elles swiche as men dye or peynte.
Colours of rethoryk ben me to queynte;
My spirit feleth noght of swich matere,
But if yow list, my tale shul ye here.

The Prologue to the Franklin's Tale

The noble Bretons of olden days composed stories about many
adventures, put into rhyme in the earliest Breton language. They
sang these tales to the accompaniment of their musical instruments,
or else read them for their own pleasure. There is one that I recall
that I will relate with as good a will as I can. But, Sirs, since I
am an unlearned man, I must, before I begin, first beg you to
excuse my rough speech. Certainly, I never learned rhetoric; what
I say must be bare and plain. I never slept on Mount Parnassus,
nor studied Marcus Tullius Cicero. There is no doubt that I know
none of the colours of speech except such colours as grow in a
meadow, or else such as men dye or paint. The colours of rhetoric
are difficult to me; my spirit has no feeling for such matters. But
if you wish, you shall hear my tale.

The Frankeleyns Tale

   In Armorik, that called is Britayne,
Ther was a knight that loved and dide his payne
To serve a lady in his beste wyse;
And many a labour, many a greet empryse
He for his lady wroghte, er she were wonne.
For she was oon, the faireste under sonne,
And eek therto come of so heigh kinrede,
That wel unnethes dorste this knight, for drede,
Telle hir his wo, his peyne, and his distresse.
But atte laste, she, for his worthinesse, 10
And namely for his meke obeysaunce,
Hath swich a pitee caught of his penaunce,
That prively she fil of his accord
To take him for hir housbonde and hir lord,
Of swich lordshipe as men han over hir wyves;

And for to lede the more in blisse hir lyves,
Of his free wil he swoor hir as a knight,
That never in al his lyf he, day ne night,
Ne sholde up-on him take no maistrye
Agayn hir wil, ne kythe hir jalousye, 20
But hir obeye, and folwe hir wil in al
As any lovere to his lady shal;
Save that the name of soveraynetee,
That wolde he have for shame of his degree.

Here begins the Franklin's Tale
In Armorica, which Britanny is called, there was a knight who loved and strove to serve his lady to the best of his ability; he undertook many a labour, many a great enterprise, before she was won.

She was one of the fairest under the sun, and also came of such high birth that, through fear, this knight scarcely dared tell her at all of his woe, suffering and distress.

However, in the end, because of his true worth and especially because of his humble deference, she took pity on his sufferings; she secretly agreed to take him for her husband and her lord, such lordship as men have over their wives.

In order that they might live their lives in greater happiness, he swore, as a knight, of his own free will, that he would never in all his life, day or night, take upon himself domination against her will, or show jealousy, but obey and follow her will in all things as any lover should for his lady, except that, out of regard for his position, he would have the name of sovereignty.

She thanked him, and with ful greet humblesse
She seyde, 'sire, sith of your gentillesse
Ye profre me to have so large a reyne,
Ne wolde never god bitwixe us tweyne,
As in my gilt, were outher werre or stryf.
Sir, I wol be your humble trewe wyf,   30
Have heer my trouthe, til that myn herte breste.'
Thus been they bothe in quiete and in reste.

   For o thing, sires, saufly dar I seye,
That frendes everich other moot obeye,
If they wol longe holden companye.
Love wol nat ben constreyned by maistrye;
Whan maistrie comth, the god of love anon
Beteth hise winges, and farewel! he is gon!
Love is a thing as any spirit free;
Wommen of kinde desiren libertee,   40
And nat to ben constreyned as a thral;
And so don men, if I soth seyen shal.
Loke who that is most pacient in love,
He is at his avantage al above.
Pacience is an heigh vertu certeyn;
For it venquisseth, as thise clerkes seyn,
Thinges that rigour sholde never atteyne.
For every word men may nat chyde or pleyne.
Lerneth to suffre, or elles, so moot I goon,
Ye shul it lerne, wher-so ye wole or noon.   50
For in this world, certein, ther no wight is,
That he ne dooth or seith som-tyme amis.
Ire, siknesse, or constellacioun,
Wyn, wo, or chaunginge of complexioun
Causeth ful ofte to doon amis or speken.
On every wrong a man may nat be wreken;
After the tyme, moste be temperaunce
To every wight that can on governaunce.
And therfore hath this wyse worthy knight,
To live in ese, suffrance hir bihight,   60
And she to him ful wisly gan to swere
That never sholde ther be defaute in here.

She thanked him and said with great humility: 'Sir, since with your nobility you offer me so free a reign, I would to God that there may never be war or strife through my fault. I, sir, will be your meek and true wife till my heart bursts. Take here my pledge.'

So were they both in peace and in repose. For there is one thing, sirs, that I can safely say: friends must obey each other if they wish to be together for long. Love will not be kept in restraint by domination. When domination comes, the god of love at once beats his wings and, farewell, he is off! Love is a thing as free as any spirit. By nature women desire freedom, and not to be kept under restraint like slaves. And so, to tell you truly, do men. He that is most patient in love has the advantage in all things. Truly, patience is a great virtue, for it conquers, as those scholars say, things that severity will never subdue. Men must not chide or reproach at every word; learn to suffer, or else, as I hope to live, you will have to learn it later, whether you wish to or not. For sure, in this world there is no being that never does nor says anything wrong. Anger, sickness, the stars, wine, grief or a change of disposition so often cause one to act or speak wrongly. A man cannot be avenged for every wrong he endures. After a time, restraint must come to every man that governs (himself). Therefore, for peace of life, this wise, worthy knight promised her forbearance, and she swore truthfully to him, that there should never be a fault in her.

Heer may men seen an humble wys accord;
Thus hath she take hir servant and hir lord,
Servant in love, and lord in mariage;
Than was he bothe in lordship and servage;
Servage? nay, but in lordshipe above,
Sith he hath bothe his lady and his love;
His lady, certes, and his wyf also,
The which that lawe of love acordeth to,   70
And whan he was in this prosperitee,
Hoom with his wyf he gooth to his contree,
Nat fer fro Penmark, ther his dwelling was,
Wher-as he liveth in blisse and in solas.

Who coude telle, but he had wedded be,
The joye, the ese, and the prosperitee
That is bitwixe an housbonde and his wyf?
A yeer and more lasted this blisful lyf,
Til that the knight of which I speke of thus,
That of Kayrrud was cleped Arveragus,   80
Shoop him to goon, and dwelle a yeer or tweyne
In Engelond, that cleped was eek Briteyne,
To seke in armes worship and honour;
For al his lust he sette in swich labour;
And dwelled ther two yeer, the book seith thus.

Here we may see a humble and wise agreement; thus has she taken a servant and a lord, servant in love and lord in marriage. Then he was both lord and in servitude. Servitude? No, but above all lord, for he had both his lady and his love; for sure, his lady and his wife as well, a state to which the law of love agrees. When he was in this happy state he went home with his wife to his own country where his home was, not far from Penmarc'h, where he lived in happiness and comfort.

Unless he has been married, who can tell of the joy, the comfort, the happy state that exists between husband and wife? This blissful life lasted for a year and more, until the knight of whom I speak, who was called Arveragus of Kayrrud arranged to go and spend a year or two in England, then called Britain, to seek reputation and honour in arms. All his heart he put into this task and dwelt there, so the book says, for two years.

Now wol I stinte of this Arveragus,
And speken I wole of Dorigene his wyf,
That loveth hir housbonde as hir hertes lyf.
For his absence wepeth she and syketh,
As doon thise noble wyves whan hem lyketh. 90
She moorneth, waketh, wayleth, fasteth, pleyneth;
Desyr of his presence hir so distreyneth,
That al this wyde world she sette at noght.
Hir frendes, whiche that knewe hir hevy thoght,
Conforten hir in al that ever they may;
They prechen hir, they telle hir night and day,
That causelees she sleeth hir-self, allas!
And every confort possible in this cas
They doon to hir with al hir bisinesse,
Al for to make hir leve hir hevinesse. 100

By proces, as ye knowen everichoon,
Men may so longe graven in a stoon,
Til som figure ther-inne emprented be.
So longe han they conforted hir, til she
Receyved hath, by hope and by resoun,
Th'emprenting of hir consolacioun,
Thurgh which hir grete sorwe gan aswage;
She may nat alwey duren in swich rage.
And eek Arveragus, in al this care,
Hath sent hir lettres hoom of his welfare, 110
And that he wol come hastily agayn;
Or elles hadde this sorwe hir herte slayn.
Hir freendes saw hir sorwe gan to slake,
And prevede hir on knees, for goddes sake,
To come and romen hir in companye,
Awey to dryve hir derke fantasye.
And finally, she graunted that requeste;
For wel she saugh that it was for the beste.

Now will I leave Arveragus for a time, and speak of his wife, Dorigen, who loves her husband as the life of her heart. During his absence, as noble wives will when it pleases them, she weeps and sighs. She mourns, lies awake, wails, does not eat, laments. Her desire for his company so torments her that she cares nought for the whole wide world. Knowing her heavy thoughts, her friends comfort her as best as they could. They exhort her, telling her, night and day, that she is killing herself for nothing. Diligently they offer every possible comfort in her state to try and lighten her burden.

Gradually, as everyone knows, men can engrave a stone until an image is imprinted upon it. They comforted her for so long until she received an imprint of their consolations through hope and common sense which calmed her great sorrow, she could not live in such a state of torment for ever.

Also, in all this anxiety Arveragus sent letters home with good news of himself, saying he would speedily return. But for this, this sorrow would have killed her.

When her friends saw that her sorrow was abating, they begged her on their knees for God's sake to come and walk with them and drive her sombre ideas away. Finally, for she saw that it was for the best, she granted their request.

Now stood hir castel faste by the see,
And often with hir freendes walketh she   120
Hir to disporte up-on the bank an heigh,
Wher-as she many a ship and barge seigh
Seilinge hir cours, wher-as hem liste go;
But than was that a parcel of hir wo.
For to hir-self ful ofte 'allas!' seith she,
'Is ther no ship, of so manye as I see,
Wol bringen hom my lord? than were myn herte
Al warisshed of his bittre peynes smerte.'

Another tyme ther wolde she sitte and thinke,
And caste hir eyen dounward fro the brinke.   130
But whan she saugh the grisly rokkes blake,
For verray fere so wolde hir herte quake,
That on hir feet she mighte hir noght sustene.
Than wolde she sitte adoun upon the grene,
And pitously in-to the see biholde,
And seyn right thus, with sorweful sykes colde:

'Eterne god, that thurgh thy purveyaunce
Ledest the world by certein governaunce,
In ydel, as men seyn, ye no-thing make;
But, lord, thise grisly feendly rokkes blake,   140
That semen rather a foul confusioun
Of werk than any fair creacioun
Of swich a parfit wys god and a stable,
Why han ye wroght this werk unresonable?
For by this werk, south, north, ne west, ne eest,
Ther nis y-fostred man, ne brid, ne beest;
It dooth no good, to my wit, but anoyeth.
See ye nat, lord, how mankinde it destroyeth?
An hundred thousand bodies of mankinde
Han rokkes slayn, al be they nat in minde,   150
Which mankinde is so fair part of thy werk
That thou it madest lyk to thyn owene merk.

Now, her castle stood close by the sea. Often she walked with her friends to enjoy herself along the high cliff. There, she saw many a ship and barque sailing their desired course. But this became part and parcel of her sorrow, for she often said to herself: 'Alas, is there no ship among the many that will bring my lord home? Then my heart would be quite cured of the smart of this bitter pain.'

At other times, she would sit and think and cast her eyes over the edge of the cliff. When she saw the terrible black rocks her heart would so quake with fear that she could not have stood on her feet. She would then sit down on the grass and gaze piteously at the sea, and with chilling sorrowful sighs say this:

'Eternal God, who through thy providence rulest the world by sure government; as men say thou createst nothing in vain. But, Lord, these fiendish, terrible black rocks seem more a foul disorder than any beautiful creation of a perfect, wise, unchanging God. Why hast thou wrought this purposeless work? For through this work no man, bird or beast is fostered; south, north, east or west. To my mind it does no good but only harm. Lord, dost thou not see how it destroys mankind? The bodies of a hundred thousand men have been slain by these rocks; although they are forgotten, men that were so fair a part of thy work, for thou created them in thine own image.

Than semed it ye hadde a greet chiertee
Toward mankinde; but how than may it be
That ye swiche menes make it to destroyen,
Whiche menes do no good, but ever anoyen?
I woot wel clerkes wol seyn, as hem leste,
By arguments, that al is for the beste,
Though I ne can the causes nat y-know.
But thilke god, that made wind to blowe,   160
As kepe my lord! this my conclusioun;
To clerkes lete I al disputisoun.
But wolde god that alle thise rokkes blake
Were sonken in-to helle for his sake!
Thise rokkes sleen myn herte for the fere.'

Thus wolde she seyn, with many a pitous tere.
    Hir freendes sawe that it was no disport
To romen by the see, but disconfort;
And shopen for to pleyen somwher elles.
They leden hir by riveres and by welles,   170
And eek in othere places delitables;
They dauncen, and they pleyen at ches and tables.

    So on a day, right in the morwe-tyde,
Un-to a gardin that was ther bisyde,
In which that they had maad hir ordinaunce
Of vitaille and of other purveyaunce,
They goon and pleye hem al the longe day.
And this was on the sixte morwe of May,
Which May had peynted with his softe shoures
This gardin ful of leves and of floures.   180
And craft of mannes hand so curiously
Arrayed hadde this gardin, trewely,
That never was ther gardin of swich prys,
But-if it were the verray paradys.
Th' odour of floures and the fresshe sighte
Wolde han maad any herte for to lighte
That ever was born, but-if to gret siknesse,
Or to gret sorwe helde it in distresse;
So ful it was of beautee with plesaunce.

Then, it seemed thou hadst a great love for mankind, but how can it be that thou createst such means to destroy it, means that do no good but always harm? I know well that priests will say, as they like to in argument, that all is for the best, although I cannot know the reasons. But let the same God who made the wind blow, preserve my lord! This is my conclusion, I leave arguments to the priests. But would to God that all these black rocks were sunk into hell for Arveragus' sake. These rocks kill my heart with fear.'

She would speak in this way shedding many a pitiful tear. Her friends saw that to roam by the sea was no recreation for her, but distress; and they planned amusements elsewhere. They took her to rivers, springs and other delightful spots. They danced and played chess and backgammon.

So one day, early in the morning, they went into a garden nearby where they had prepared food and other provisions and they amused themselves all through the day. This was on the sixth morning of May. May had painted with her gentle showers this garden full of leaves and flowers, and man's art had so skilfully laid out this garden that there never was truly a garden of such excellence unless it were paradise itself. The scent of the flowers and the gay sight would have lightened any heart ever born, unless great sickness or sorrow kept it in distress, for it was so full of beauty and delight.

At-after diner gonne they to daunce,
And singe also, save Dorigen allone,
Which made alwey hir compleint and hir mone;
For she ne saugh him on the daunce go,
That was hir housbonde and hir love also,
But nathelees she moste a tyme abyde,
And with good hope lete hir sorwe slyde,

   Up-on this daunce, amonges othere men,
Daunced a squyer biforen Dorigen,
That fressher was and jolyer of array,
As to my doom, than is the monthe of May.   200
He singeth, daunceth, passinge any man
That is, or was, sith that the world bigan.
Ther-with he was, if men sholde him discryve,
Oon of the beste faringe man on-lyve;
Yong, strong, right vertuous, and riche and wys,
And wel biloved, and holden in gret prys.

After dinner they danced and sang, except for Dorigen who lamented all the time, bewailing (the fact) that she did not see the man who was her husband, and also her love, in the dance. Nevertheless she must endure for a time and let sorrow diminish with hope.

Among the other men dancing before her was a Squire, brighter and more finely arrayed I think than the month of May itself. He sings, dances, surpassing any man that lives or lived since the world began. In effect, if one may describe him, he was one of the handsomest alive; young, strong, truly accomplished, rich, wise, well-loved and held in great esteem.

And shortly, if the sothe I tellen shal,
Unwiting of this Dorigen at al,
This lusty squyer, servant to Venus,
Which that y-cleped was Aurelius, 210
Had loved hir best of any creature
Two yeer and more, as was his aventure,
But never dorste he telle hir his grevaunce;
With-outen coppe he drank al his penaunce.
He was despeyred, no-thing dorste he seye,
Save in his songes somwhat wolde he wreye
His wo, as in a general compleyning;
He seyde he lovede, and was biloved nothing.
Of swich matere made he manye layes,
Songes, compleintes, roundels, virelayes, 220
How that he dorste nat his sorwe telle,
But languissheth, as a furie dooth in helle;
And dye he moste, he seyde, as dide Ekko
For Narcisus, that dorste nat telle hir wo.
In other manere than ye here me seye,
Ne dorste he nat to hir his wo biwreye;
Save that, paraventure, som-tyme at daunces,
Ther yonge folk kepen hir observaunces,
It may wel be he loked on hir face
In swich a wyse, as man that asketh grace; 230
But no-thing wiste she of his entente.

Briefly, to tell you the truth, all unknown to Dorigen, this vigorous squire, a servant of Venus whose name was Aurelius, was fated to have loved her best of all beings for two years or more and had never dared tell her his distress. He drank the cup of suffering to the dregs. He was in despair, never daring to say a thing, except by revealing his woes in his songs as though in a general lament. He said he loved, but that he was not loved at all. On such matters he composed many lays, songs, complaints and ballads about the fact that he never dared relate his sorrows, but languished like a fury in hell, and he said he must die like Echo for Narcissus, not daring to speak her sorrow. But, as you heard me say, he did not dare in any other way reveal his suffering to her. Except that, by chance on occasion at dances, when young people keep to the customs, it may well be that he gazed at her face in the way a man begs for mercy, but she nothing at all of his meaning.

Nathelees, it happed, er they thennes wente,
By-cause that he was hir neighebour,
And was a man of worship and honour,
And hadde y-knowen him of tyme yore,
They fille in speche; and forth more and more
Un-to his purpos drough Aurelius,
And whan he saugh his tyme, he seyde thus:
   'Madame,' quod he, 'by god that this world made,
So that I wiste it mighte your herte glade,   240
I wolde, that day that you Arveragus
Wente over the see, that I, Aurelius,
Had went ther never I sholde have come agayn:
For wel I woot my service is in vayn.
My guerdon is but bresting of myn herte;
Madame, reweth upon my peynes smerte;
For with a word ye may me sleen or save,
Heer at your feet god wolde that I were grave!
I ne have as now no leyser more to seye;
Have mercy, swete, or ye wol do me deye!'   250

Nevertheless, before they left there, it came about that they began to talk because he was her neighbour, a man of reputation and honour whom she had known for a long time. Continually, Aurelius came gradually nearer to his purpose, and when he saw an opportune moment he spoke: 'Madam, by God who made the world, if I had known it would gladden your heart, it would have been my wish that on the day your Arveragus went overseas, that I, Aurelius, had gone there never to return, for I know that my devotion is in vain. My reward is merely the breaking of my heart. Madam, have pity on my bitter suffering for you can slay or save me with one word. I would to God that I were buried here at your feet. Now, I have no time to say more, have mercy, my love, or you will make me die.'

    She gan to loke up-on Aurelius:
'Is this your wil,' quod she, 'and sey ye thus?
Never erst,' quod she, 'ne wiste I what ye mente.
But now, Aurelie, I knowe your entente,
By thilke god that yaf me soule and lyf,
Ne shal I never been untrewe wyf
In word ne werk, as fer as I have wit;
I wol ben his to whom that I am knit;
Tak this for fynal answer as of me.'

But after that in pley thus seyde she: 260
    'Aurelie,' quod she, 'by heighe god above,
Yet wolde I graunte yow to been your love,
Sin I yow see so pitously complayne;
Loke what day that, endelong Britayne,
Ye remoeve alle the rokkes, stoon by stoon,
That they ne lette ship ne boot to goon –
I seye, whan ye han maad the coost so clene
Of rokkes, that there nis no stoon y-sene,
Than wol I love yow best of any man;
Have heer my trouthe in al that ever I can.'   270
'Is ther non other grace in yow?' quod he.

'No, by that lord,' quod she, 'that maked me!
For wel I woot that it shal never bityde.
Lat swiche folies out of your herte slyde.
What deyntee sholde a man han in his lyf
For to go love another mannes wyf,
That hath hir body whan so that him lyketh?'
    Aurelius ful ofte sore syketh;
Wo was Aurelie, whan that he this herde,
And with a sorweful herte he thus answerde: 280
    'Madame,' quod he, 'this were an inpossible!
Than moot I dye of sodein deth horrible.'
And with that word he turned him anoon.

She gazed at Aurelius: 'Do you mean this and speak it? I never knew before what you meant. But now, Aurelius, that I know your desire, by God who gave me a soul and life, I will never knowingly be an unfaithful wife in word or deed. I will be his to whom I am bound. Accept this as my final answer.'

But after this, she said jokingly: 'Aurelius, by the High God above, since I see you lament so sorrowfully, I would yet agree to be your love on the day when you remove from the whole length of Britanny all the rocks, stone by stone, so that they hinder no boat or ship on its way. When you have made the coast so free of rocks that there is not a stone to be seen, I say that then I will love you better than any other man. As I can give it, you can take my word for this.'

'Is there no further pity in you?' he asked.

'No,' she replied, 'by the Lord that created me. For I know well that it will never come to pass. Cast out this madness from your heart. What pleasure can a man have in life by loving the wife of another man who can have her body when he pleases?'

Aurelius uttered many painful sighs. He was sad when he heard this and answered with a sorrowful heart: 'Madam this is impossible, so I must die a sudden, horrible death.'

And with these words, he left immediately.

Tho come hir othere freendes many oon,
And in the aleyes romeden up and doun,
And no-thing wiste of this conclusioun,
But sodeinly bigonne revel newe
Til that the brighte sonne loste his hewe;
For th'orisonte hath reft the sonne his light;
This is as muche to seye as it was night.   290
And hoom they goon in joye and in solas,
Save only wrecche Aurelius, allas!
He to his hous is goon with sorweful herte;
He seeth he may nat from his deeth asterte.
Him semed that he felte his herte colde;
Up to the hevene his handes he gan holde,
And on his knowes bare he sette him doun,
And in his raving seyde his orisoun.
For verray wo out of his wit he breyde.
He niste what he spak, but thus he seyde;   300
With pitous herte his pleynt hath he bigonne
Un-to the goddes, and first un-to the sonne:

He seyde, 'Appollo, god and governour
Of every plaunte, herbe, tree and flour,
That yevest, after thy declinacioun,
To ech of hem his tyme and his sesoun,
As thyn herberwe chaungeth lowe or hye,
Lord Phebus, cast thy merciable yë
On wrecche Aurelie, which that am but lorn.
Lo, lord! my lady hath my deeth y-sworn   310
With-oute gilt, but thy benignitee
Upon my dedly herte have som pitee!
For wel I woot, lord Phebus, if yow lest,
Ye may me helpen, save my lady, best.
Now voucheth sauf that I may yow devyse
How that I may been holpe and in what wyse.

Then her other friends came, wandering up and down the garden paths, knowing nothing of this bargain. At once new revels began, until the time the bright sun lost its glow, for the horizon bereft the sun of its light – which is as much as saying that it was night! Home they went in happiness and content, except, alas, poor Aurelius! Sorrowful at heart he went home. He saw he could not escape death; it seemed to him his heart grew cold. He held his hands up to heaven and knelt down on his bare knees and wildly said his prayers. His very sorrow put him out of his mind, he did not know what he was saying but spoke like this. With pitiful heart he began his lament to the Gods, firstly to the sun.

He said: 'Apollo, god and ruler of every plant, herb, tree and flower, who, according to thy declination givest to each of them its time and season as thy position in the sky changes from low to high, Lord Phoebus cast thy merciful eye on this wretch Aurelius who am completely lost. Behold, Lord, my lady has sworn my death through no fault of mine, but in thy mercy take some pity on my dying heart. For I know well, Lord Phoebus, that if thou wilt thou canst help me better than anyone except my lady. Now allow me to set out for you now and in what way I could be helped.

Your blisful suster, Lucina the shene,
That of the see is chief goddesse and quene,
Though Neptunus have deitee in the see,
Yet emperesse aboven him is she: 320
Ye knowen wel, lord, that right as hir desyr
Is to be quiked and lightned of your fyr,
For which she folweth yow ful bisily,
Right so the see desyreth naturelly
To folwen hir, as she that is goddesse
Bothe in the see and riveres more and lesse.
Wherfore, lord Phebus, this is my requeste –
Do this miracle, or do myn herte breste –
That now, next at this opposicioun,
Which in the signe shal be of the Leoun,   330
As preyeth hir so greet a flood to bringe,
That fyve fadme at the leeste it overspringe
The hyeste rokke in Armorik Briteyne;
And lat this flood endure yeres tweyne;
Than certes to my lady may I seye:
"Holdeth your heste, the rokkes been aweye."
    Lord Phebus, dooth this miracle for me;
Preye hir she go no faster cours than ye;
I seye, preyeth your suster that she go
No faster cours than ye thise yeres two.   340
Than shal she been evene atte fulle alway,
And spring-flood laste bothe night and day.
And, but she vouche-sauf in swiche manere
To graunte me my sovereyn lady dere,
Prey hir to sinken every rok adoun
In-to hir owene derke regioun
Under the ground, ther Pluto dwelleth inne,
Or never-mo shal I my lady winne.
Thy temple in Delphos wol I barefoot seke;
Lord Phebus, see the teres on my cheke,   350
And of my peyne have som compassioun.'

Thy blessed sister, Lucina the fair, who is chief goddess and queen of the sea (although Neptune has deity in the sea, yet is she empress over him) – thou knowest well, Lord, that just as her desire is to be kindled and lit by thy fire, for which purpose she follows thee eagerly, in the same way the sea naturally desires to follow her for she is goddess both in the sea and in rivers great and small.

Wherefore, Lord Phoebus, this is my request – perform this miracle or break my heart – that at the next opposition, which will be in the sign of Leo, pray her to bring so great a tide that it will submerge the highest rock in Armorica Brittany to a depth of at least five fathoms, and let this tide last for two years that I may then say with certainty to my lady, "Keep your word, the rocks are gone". Lord Phoebus, work the miracle for me. Pray her to go no faster course than thou, I say, pray thy sister that she go no faster course than thee for these two years, then she will always be at full moon and the spring tide will last both night and day. Unless she promises to grant me my dear sovereign lady in that way, pray her to sink each rock down into her own dark regions underground wherein Pluto dwells, or I will never win my lady. I will go barefoot to thy temple in Delphos, Lord Phoebus. See the tears on my cheeks and have pity on my suffering.'

And with that word in swowne he fil adoun,
And longe tyme he lay forth in a traunce.
   His brother, which that knew of his penaunce,
Up caughte him and to bedde he hath him broght.
Dispeyred in this torment and this thoght
Lete I this woful creature lye;
Chese he, for me, whether he wol live or dye.

   Arveragus, with hele and greet honour,
As he that was of chivalrye the flour, 360
Is comen hoom, and othere worthy men.
O blisful artow now, thou Dorigen,
That hast thy lusty housbonde in thyne armes,
The fresshe knight, the worthy man of armes,
That loveth thee, as his owene hertes lyf.
No-thing list him to been imaginatyf
If any wight had spoke, whyl he was oute,
To hire of love; he hadde of it no doute.
He noght entendeth to no swich matere,
But daunceth, justeth, maketh hir good chere;
And thus in joye and blisse I lete hem dwelle, 370
And of the syke Aurelius wol I telle.

With these words he swooned and lay there in a trance for a long time.

His brother, who knew of his suffering, took him up and brought him to his bed. I will leave this piteous creature lying there despairing in this torment. For my part let him choose whether he live or die.

In health and great honour, like the flower of chivalry he was, Arveragus has come home with other worthy men. How happy are you now, Dorigen, holding your vigorous husband in your arms, that bold knight, worthy man of arms, who loves you as his own life. He does not imagine at all that any man has spoken to her of love while he was away. Of that he had no fear in his mind at all. He thinks nothing of such matters but dances, jousts and entertains her. So in joy and happiness I will leave him and tell of the sick man Aurelius.

In langour and in torment furious
Two yeer and more lay wrecche Aurelius,
Er any foot he mighte on crthe goon;
Ne confort in this tyme hadde he noon,
Save of his brother, which that was a clerk;
He knew of al this wo and al this werk.
For to non other creature certeyn
Of this matere he dorste no word seyn.   380
Under his brest he bar it more secree
Than ever dide Pamphilus for Galathee.
His brest was hool, with-oute for to sene,
But in his herte ay was the arwe kene.
And wel ye knowe that of a sursanure
In surgerye is perilous the cure,
But men mighte touche the arwe, or come thereby.
His brother weep and wayled prively,
Til atte laste him fil in remembraunce,
That whyl he was at Orliens in Fraunce,   390
As yonge clerkes, that been likerous
To reden artes that been curious,
Seken in every halke and every herne
Particuler sciences for to lerne,
He him remembred that, upon a day,
At Orliens in studie a book he say
Of magik naturel, which his felawe,
That was that tyme a bacheler of lawe,
Al were he ther to lerne another craft,
Had prively upon his desk y-laft;   400
Which book spak muchel of the operaciouns,
Touchinge the eighte and twenty mansiouns
That longen to the mone, and swich folye,
As in our dayes is nat worth a flye;
For holy chirches feith in our bileve
Ne suffreth noon illusion us to greve.

For two years or more wretched Aurelius lay languishing in raging torment before he put foot upon the ground. He received no comfort during this time except from his brother who was a scholar. He knew of all this woe and trouble. To be sure, he dared not say a word of this to any person. He kept it to himself more secretly than ever did Pamphilus about Galatea. Outwardly his breast was whole, but there was a sharp arrow in his heart. And you know well that in surgery a surface healing of a wound threatens the cure unless men might reach the arrow or get near it. His brother wept and sorrowed secretly, till at last he remembered that when he was at Orleans in France, eager as young scholars are to study occult art, and seek in every nook and cranny to learn extraordinary knowledge, he called to mind that one day in Orleans during his studies he saw a book about Natural Magic which a comrade, a bachelor of law then, although later he was to learn another craft, had secretly left on his desk. This book related much about the workings concerning the twenty-eight mansions of the moon, and such folly as in our day is not worth a fly – for the faith of Holy Church in our creed allows no illusions to trouble us.

And whan this book was in his remembraunce,
Anon for joye his herte gan to daunce,
And to him-self he seyde prively:
'My brother shal be warisshed hastily;   410
For I am siker that ther be sciences,
By whiche men make diverse apparences
Swiche as thise subtile tregetoures pleye.
For ofte at festes have I wel herd seye,
That tregetours, with-inne an halle large,
Have maad come in a water and a barge,
And in the halle rowen up and doun.
Somtyme hath semed come a grim leoun;
And somtyme floures springe as in a mede;
Somtyme a vyne, and grapes whyte and rede;   420
Somtyme a castel, al of lym and stoon;
And whan hem lyked, voyded it anoon.
Thus semed it to every mannes sighte.
   Now than conclude I thus, that if I mighte
At Orliens som old felawe y-finde,
That hadde this mones mansions in minde,
Or other magik naturel above,
He sholde wel make my brother han his love.
For with an apparence a clerk may make
To mannes sighte, that alle the rokkes blake   430
Of Britaigne weren y-voyded everichon,
And shippes by the brinke comen and gon,
And in swich forme endure a day or two;
Than were my brother warisshed of his wo.
Than moste she nedes holden hir biheste,
Or elles he shal shame hir atte leste.'

When he recalled this book, his heart at once began to dance for joy and he said to himself privately:

'My brother will be cured quickly, for I am certain there are sciences by which men can create various illusions such as these clever magicians we hear about perform. I have indeed heard tell how often at feasts magicians have created water and a barge that was rowed up and down. Sometimes a grim lion seemed to appear, sometimes flowers to spring up as in a meadow, sometimes a vine and red and white grapes, sometimes a castle all in stone, and when they wished, they made it disappear at once. So it seemed in everyone's eyes. So I conclude that if I could find at Orleans some old comrade who remembered these mansions of the moon or, in addition, other natural magic, he could well arrange for my brother to obtain the one he loves. Since with an illusion a scholar can make to man's eyes each and every one of the rocks of Brittany disappear and ships come and go along the shore and remain thus for a time, then my brother would be cured of his ill, then will she have to keep her promise or else at least he will put her to shame.'

What sholde I make a lenger tale of this?
Un-to his brothers bed he comen is,
And swich confort he yaf him for to gon
To Orliens, that he up stirte anon,   440
And on his wey forthward thanne is he fare,
In hope for to ben lissed of his care.
    Whan they were come almost to that citee,
But-if it were a two furlong or three,
A yong clerk rominge by him-self they mette,
Which that in Latin thriftily hem grette,
And after that he seyde a wonder thing:
'I knowe,' quod he, 'the cause of your coming';
And er they ferther any fote wente,
He tolde hem al that was in hir entente.   450
    This Briton clerk him asked of felawes
The whiche that he had knowe in olde dawes;
And he answerde him that they dede were,
For which he weep ful ofte many a tere.

    Doun of his hors Aurelius lighte anon,
And forth with this magicien is he gon
Hoom to his hous, and made hem wel at ese.
Hem lakked no vitaille that mighte hem plese;
So wel arrayed hous as ther was oon
Aurelius in his lyf saugh never noon.   460
    He shewed him, er he wente to sopeer,
Forestes, parkes ful of wilde deer;
Ther saugh he hertes with hir hornes hye,
The gretteste that ever were seyn with yë.
He saugh of hem an hondred slayn with houndes,
And somme with arwes blede of bittre woundes.
He saugh, whan voided were thise wilde deer,
Thise fauconers upon a fair river,
That with hir haukes han the heron slayn.

Why should I make a longer tale of all this? He came to his brother's bed and gave him such encouragement that immediately he started up to go to Orleans, and straightaway went on his way in the hope of being relieved of his cares.

When they had almost arrived at that city, with but two or three furlongs to go, they met a young scholar strolling by himself who greeted them politely in Latin and afterwards said a strange thing:

'I know,' he said, 'the reason for your coming,' and before they took another step, he told them in full their intentions.

This Breton scholar asked him about fellow students he had known in olden days, and he answered him that they were dead for which he often shed many a tear.

At once, Aurelius dismounted from his horse and went with this magician to his house where he made them perfectly at ease. They lacked no food that might please them. Never was there so finely ordered a house; in his life Aurelius had never seen one like it.

Before they went to supper he showed him forests, parks full of wild deer, there they saw harts with high antlers greater than ever seen by human eye. He saw a hundred of them killed by hounds and some bleeding from bitter arrow wounds. When these wild deer disappeared they saw on a river falconers who killer heron with their hawks.

Tho saugh he knightes justing in a playn;   470
And after this, he dide him swich plesaunce,
That he him shewed his lady on a daunce
On which him-self he daunced, as him thoughte.
And whan this maister, that this magik wroughte,
Saugh it was tyme, he clapte his handes two,
And farewel! al our revel was ago.
And yet remoeved they never out of the hous,
Whyl they saugh al this sighte merveillous,
But in his studie, ther-as his bookes be,
They seten stille, and no wight but they three.   480

    To him this maister called his squyer,
And seyde him thus: 'is redy our soper?
Almost an houre it is, I undertake,
Sith I yow bad our soper for to make,
Whan that thise worthy men wenten with me
In-to my studie, ther-as my bookes be.'
    'Sire,' quod this squyer, 'whan it lyketh yow,
It is al redy, though ye wol right now.'
'Go we than soupe,' quod he, 'as for the beste;
This amorous folk som-tyme mote han reste.'   490

    At-after soper fille they in tretee,
What somme sholde this maistres guerdon be,
To remoeven all the rokkes of Britayne,
And eek from Gerounde to the mothe of Sayne.
    He made it straunge, and swoor, so god him save,
Lasse than a thousand pound he wolde nat have,
Ne gladly for that somme he wolde nat goon.

Then they saw knights jousting on a plain, and after this he gave great pleasure by showing his lady in a dance in which it seemed he also took part. When the master who wrought the magic saw that it was time, he clapped his hands and, farewell, all our revels were gone! Yet they had never moved out of the house while watching this marvellous sight but had sat quiet, none but they three present in his study where his books were.

This master called his squire to him and said: 'Is our supper ready? I guarantee it is almost an hour since I ordered you to make supper when these distinguished men came with me into my study where my books are.'

'Sir, when it pleases you, it is all ready,' the squire replied, 'even if you want it at once.'

'Then,' said he, 'let us go to supper, that's the best thing to do, for these amorous folk must rest sometime!'

After supper they began to discuss what sum should be this master's reward for removing all the rocks of Brittany, right from the Gironde to the mouth of the Seine. He made difficulties and swore, may God save him, that he would not take less than a thousand pounds, and he would not even go willingly for that sum.

Aurelius, with blisful herte anoon,
Answerde thus, 'fy on a thousand pound!
This wyde world, which that men seye is round,   500
I wolde it yeve, if I were lord of it.
This bargayn is ful drive, for we ben knit.
Ye shal be payed trewely, by my trouthe!
But loketh now, for no necligence or slouthe,
Ye tarie us heer no lenger than to-morwe.'
    'Nay,' quod this clerk, 'have heer my feith to borwe.'
    To bedde is goon Aurelius whan him leste,
And wel ny al that night he hadde his reste;
What for his labour and his hope of blisse,
His woful herte of penaunce hadde a lisse.   510

Upon the morwe, whan that it was day,
To Britaigne toke they the righte way,
Aurelius, and this magicien bisyde,
And been descended ther they wolde abyde;
And this was, as the bokes me remembre,
The colde frosty seson of Decembre.
    Phebus wex old, and hewed lyk latoun,
That in his hote declinacioun
Shoon as the burned gold with stremes brighte;
But now in Capricorn adoun he lighte,   520
Wher-as he shoon ful pale, I dar wel seyn.
The bittre frostes, with the sleet and reyn,
Destroyed hath the grene in every yerd.
Janus sit by the fyr, with double berd,
And drinketh of his bugle-horn the wyn.
Biforn him stant braun of the tusked swyn,
And 'Nowel' cryeth every lusty man.

With a happy heart Aurelius at once replied, 'Fie on a thousand pounds! If I were master of it, I would give the wide world which men say is round. The bargain's made for we are agreed. On my word, you shall be paid truly. But listen now, through no negligence or sloth will you delay us here longer than tomorrow.'

'No,' replied the scholar, 'take my promise as a pledge.'

When it pleased him, Aurelius went to bed and slept nearly all that night, for with his exertions and his hopes of happiness his sad heart had relief from suffering.

In the morning, when it was day, Aurelius and this magician with him took the direct way to Brittany and put up where they were to stay. It was, as books remind me, the cold frosty season of December. Phoebus (i.e *the sun*) grew old and copper-coloured which in his hot declension shone like burnished gold with bright beams. Now he settles in Capricorn, where I dare indeed to say, he shone palely. The bitter frosts with sleet and rain have destroyed the green in every garden. Janus sits by the fire with double beard and drinks his wine from his bugle-horn, and before him stand the carcasses of tusky swine and every lusty man cries, 'Noël!'

    Aurelius, in al that ever he can,
Doth to his maister chere and reverence,
And preyeth him to doon.his diligence   530
To bringen him out of his peynes smerte,
Or with a swerd that he wolde slitte his herte.

    This subtil clerk swich routhe had of this man,
That night and day he spedde him that he can,
To wayte a tyme of his conclusioun;
This is to seye, to make illusioun,
By swich an apparence or jogelrye,
I ne can no termes of astrologye,
That she and every wight sholde wene and seye,
That of Britaigne the rokkes were aweye,   540
Or elles they were sonken under grounde.
So atte laste he hath his tyme y-founde
To maken his japes and his wrecchednesse
Of swich a supersticious cursednesse.
His tables Toletanes forth he broght,
Ful wel corrected, ne ther lakked noght,
Neither his collect ne his expans yeres,
Ne his rotes ne his othere geres,
As been his centres and his arguments,
And his proporcionels convenients   550
For his equacions in every thing.
And, by his eighte spere in his wirking,
He knew ful wel how fer Alnath was shove
Fro the heed of thilke fixe Aries above
That in the ninthe speere considered is;
Ful subtilly he calculed al this.

In every way he can, Aurelius gives entertainment and show of respect to this Master and begs him do his utmost to rid him of his raging agony, or he will slit his heart with a sword.

This skilful scholar took such pity on this man that night and day he hastened as much as he could awaiting the (right) time for his experiment, that is to say to create an illusion by such a conjuring trick – I don't use astrological terms – that she (Dorigen) and everyone else would imagine and say the rocks were gone from Brittany, or else had sunk underground. Thus, at last, he found the moment to perform his tricks and wretched work of such diabolic wickedness. He took out his toledo Tables, corrected so that nothing was lacking, neither his tables for calculating round and short periods, nor his tables of roots, nor his other gear, centres and angles, and his tables of proportional path for equations in all matters. By the Eighth Sphere in his calculations he knew truly how far Alnath had moved on from the head of the same fixed Aries above, which is thought to be in the Ninth Sphere. Expertly he had calculated all this.

Whan he had founde his firste mansioun,
He knew the remenant by proporcioun;
And knew the arysing of his mone weel,
And in whos face, and terme, and every-deel;   560
And knew ful weel the mones mansioun
Acordaunt to his operacioun,
And knew also his othere observaunces
For swiche illusiouns and swiche meschaunces
As hethen folk used in thilke dayes;
For which no lenger maked he delayes,
But thurgh his magik, for a wyke or tweye,
It seemed that alle the rokkes were aweye.

Aurelius, which that yet despeired is
Wher he shal han his love or fare amis,   570
Awaiteth night and day on this miracle;
And whan he knew that ther was noon obstacle,
That voided were thise rokkes everichon,
Doun to his maistres feet he fil anon,
And seyde, 'I woful wrecche, Aurelius,
Thanke yow, lord, and lady myn Venus,
That me han holpen fro my cares colde:'
And to the temple his wey forth hath he holde,
Wher-as he knew he sholde his lady see.
And whan he saugh his tyme, anon-right he,   580
With dredful herte and with ful humble chere,
Salewed hath his sovereyn lady dere:

When he had found his first 'mansion' proportionately he knew the rest, and knew the rising of the moon perfectly, in what face, terms and everything. He knew completely the moon's mansion according to his experiments, and also other customary rites for such illusions and evil customs as heathen folk used in those days. As a result he no longer delayed and through his magic it seemed for a week or two that all the rocks were gone.

Aurelius, still desperate as to whether he shall have his love or fare ill, waited night and day for this miracle. When he knew there was no obstacle, that every one of the rocks was gone, at once he fell down at the master's feet and said:

'I, woeful, wretched Aurelius, thank you Lord and my Lady Venus, who have relieved me of my fateful woes.' And straight away he made his way to the temple where he knew he would see his lady. When he saw his moment, right away with quaking heart and very humble demeanour he greeted his dear sovereign lady.

'My righte lady,' quod this woful man,
'Whom I most drede and love as I best can,
And lothest were of al this world displese,
Nere it that I for yow have swich disese,
That I moste dyen heer at your foot anon,
Noght wolde I telle how me is wo bigon;
But certes outher moste I dye or pleyne;
Ye slee me giltelees for verray peyne.   590
But of my deeth, thogh that ye have no routhe,
Avyseth yow, er that ye breke your trouthe.
Repenteth yow, for thilke god above,
Er ye me sleen by-cause that I yow love.
For, madame, wel ye woot what ye han hight;
Nat that I chalange any thing of right
Of yow my sovereyn lady, but your grace;
But in a gardin yond, at swich a place,
Ye woot right wel what ye bihighten me;
And in myn hand your trouthe plighten ye   600
To love me best, god woot, ye seyde so,
Al be that I unworthy be therto.
Madame, I speke it for the honour of yow,
More than to save myn hertes lyf right now;
I have do so as ye comanded me;
And if ye vouche-sauf, ye may go see.
Doth as yow list, have your biheste in minde,
For quik or deed, right ther ye shul me finde;
In yow lyth al, to do me live or deye; –
But wel I woot the rokkes been aweye!'   610

'My own true lady,' said this sorrowing man, 'whom I most honour, and love as best I can and would of all this world most unwillingly displease, were it not that I have such sorrow on your account that I must die here at your feet at once, I would not tell you anything of how I am oppressed with grief. But certain it is that I must die or mourn. You slay me guiltless for suffering's sake. But though you feel no pity at my death, reflect before you break your word. For the sake of God above, repent before you kill me for loving you. For you know well, Madam, what you promised. Not that I claim anything by right, my sovereign lady, but through your grace. But in yonder garden, at such a place, you know truly what you promised me and you gave your promise, your hand in mine, to love me best – God knows you said so – albeit I am unworthy. Madam, I recount it now for your honour rather than to save my life. I have done as you commanded me and, if you condescend, you may go and see. Do what you will. Keep your promise in mind, for alive or dead there you shall find me, to let me live or die lies entirely in your hands – but I know well the rocks are gone.'

He taketh his leve, and she astonied stood,
In al hir face nas a drope of blood;
She wende never han come in swich a trappe:
'Allas!' quod she, 'that ever this sholde happe!
For wende I never, by possibilitee,
That swich a monstre or merveille mighte be!
It is agayns the proces of nature':

And hoom she gooth a sorweful creature.
For verray fere unnethe may she go,
She wepeth, wailleth, al a day or two,   620
And swowneth, that it routhe was to see;
But why it was, to no wight tolde she;
For out of toune was goon Arveragus.
But to hir-self she spak, and seyde thus,
With face pale and with ful sorweful chere,
In hir compleynt, as ye shul after here:

'Allas,' quod she, 'on thee, Fortune, I pleyne,
That unwar wrapped hast me in thy cheyne;
For which, t'escape, woot I no socour
Save only deeth or elles dishonour;   630
Oon of thise two bihoveth me to chese.
But nathelees, yet have I lever lese
My lyf than of my body have a shame,
Or knowe my-selven fals, or lese my name,
And with my deth I may be quit, y-wis.
Hath ther nat many a noble wyf, er this,
And many a mayde y-slayn hir-self, allas!
Rather than with hir body doon trespas?

He took his leave and she stood astounded, her face drained of blood. Never had she expected to fall into such a trap.

'Alas!' she said, 'that ever this should have happened, for I never dreamt by any chance that such a marvellous or unnatural thing might occur. It is contrary to nature.'

She went home, a creature stricken with grief, scarcely walking for fear. She weeps and wails, throughout a day or two and swoons so that it was pitiful to all. The reason why she tells no one is that Arveragus has gone away, but she speaks to herself with pale face and sorrowful countenance in this way in her lamentations, as you shall hear now.

'Alas!' she said, 'I reproach you, Fortune, that unawares have bound me in chains from which I know no help to escape, except death or dishonour. I have to choose one of these two. But none the less I would rather lose my life than bring shame upon my body, know myself false or lose my good name. I will surely be released (from my bond) by death. Has there not been many a noble wife before this, and many a maiden, who has killed herself rather than sin with her body?

Yıs, certes, lo, thise stories beren witnesse;
Whan thretty tyraunts, ful of cursednesse,   640
Had slayn Phidoun in Athenes, atte feste,
They comanded his doghtres for t'areste,
And bringen hem biforn hem in despyt
Al naked, to fulfille hir foul delyt,
And in hir fadres blood they made hem daunce
Upon the pavement, god yeve hem mischaunce!
For which thise woful maydens, ful of drede,
Rather than they wolde lese hir maydenhede,
They prively ben stirt in-to a welle,
And dreynte hem-selven, as the bokes telle.   650
    They of Messene lete enquere and seke
Of Lacedomie fifty maydens eke,
On whiche they wolden doon hir lecherye;
But was ther noon of al that companye
That she nas slayn, and with a good entente
Chees rather for to dye than assente
To been oppressed of hir maydenhede.
Why sholde I thanne to dye been in drede?

    Lo, eek, the tiraunt Aristoclides
That loved a mayden, heet Stimphalides,   660
Whan that hir fader slayn was on a night,
Un-to Dianes temple goth she right,
And hente the image in hir handes two,
Fro which image wolde she never go.
No wight ne mighte hir handes of it arace,
Til she was slayn right in the selve place.

Truly, these stories bear witness. When thirty tyrants, full of evil, had slain Phidon at a feast in Athens, they commanded the arrest of his daughters, to be brought before them naked, contemptuously to satisfy their foul desires, making them dance in their father's blood on the paving stones, may God confound them! For which these sad maidens, fearful, rather than lose their maidenhead, secretly, as the books tell, leapt into a well and drowned themselves. Also they of Messene sought out fifty maidens of Lacedaemonia on whom they wanted to carry out their lechery, but there was not one of all that company that was not killed, and willingly chose death rather than consent to be ravished of her maidenhead. Then why should I be in fear of death?

Consider as well, the tyrant Aristoclides, who loved a maiden called Stymphalis. One night when her father was slain she went straight to the temple of Diana and seized the image in her two hands. From this image she would never let go, no man could tear it from her hands until she was slain right on the same spot.

Now sith that maydens hadden swich despyt
To been defouled with mannes foul delyt,
Wel oghte a wyf rather hir-selven slee
Than be defouled, as it thinketh me.   670
    What shal I seyn of Hasdrubales wyf,
That at Cartage birafte hir-self hir lyf?
For whan she saugh that Romayns wan the toun,
She took hir children alle, and skipte adoun
In-to the fyr, and chees rather to dye
Than any Romayn dide hir vileinye.
    Hath nat Lucresse y-slayn hir-self, allas!
At Rome, whanne she oppressed was
Of Tarquin, for hir thoughte it was a shame
To liven whan she hadde lost hir name?   680
    The sevene maydens of Milesie also
Han slayn hem-self, for verray drede and wo,
Rather than folk of Gaule hem sholde oppresse.
Mo than a thousand stories, as I gesse,
Coude I now telle as touchinge this matere.
    Whan Habradate was slayn, his wyf so dere
Hirselven slow, and leet hir blood to glyde
In Habradates woundes depe and wyde;
And seyde, 'my body, at the leeste way,
Ther shal no wight defoulen, if I may.'   690

Since maidens scorn defilement by man's foul pleasure, so ought a married woman rather kill herself, it seems to me, than be defiled. What shall I tell of Hasdrubal's wife who took her own life at Carthage? For when she saw the Romans had taken the town, she took all her children and leapt down into the flames, choosing to die rather than let any Roman violate her. Alas! Did not Lucretia kill herself at Rome when she had been raped by Tarquin, for it seemed to her shameful to live when she had lost her good name? The seven maidens of Miletus also killed themselves in true fear and sorrow rather than that the men of Gaul should ravish them. I suppose I could tell more than a thousand stories on the subject. When Abradates was slain, his dear wife killed herself and let her blood flow into his deep wide wounds and said, "at the very least no man shall defile my body if I can help it".

What sholde I mo ensamples heer-of sayn,
Sith that so manye han hem-selven slayn
Wel rather than they wolde defouled be?
I wol conclude, that it is bet for me
To sleen my-self, than been defouled thus.
I wol be trewe un-to Arveragus,
Or rather sleen my-self in som manere,
As dide Demociones doghter dere,
By-cause that she wolde nat defouled be.

O Cedasus! it is ful greet pitee,   700
To reden how thy doghtren deyde, allas!
That slowe hem-selven for swich maner cas.

As greet a pitee was it, or wel more,
The Theban mayden, that for Nichanore
Hir-selven slow, right for swich maner wo.

Another Theban mayden dide right so;
For oon of Macedoine hadde hir oppressed,
She with hir deeth hir maydenhede redressed.

What shal I seye of Nicerates wyf,
That for swich cas birafte hir-self hir lyf?   710

How trewe eek was to Alcebiades
His love, that rather for to dyen chees
Than for to suffre his body unburied be!
Lo which a wyf was Alcestè,' quod she.

'What seith Omer of gode Penalopee?
Al Grece knoweth of hir chastitee.
Pardee, of Laodomya is writen thus,
That whan at Troye was slayn Protheselaus,
No lenger wolde she live after his day.

The same of noble Porcia telle I may;   720
With-oute Brutus coude she nat live,
To whom she hadde al hool hir herte yive.

The parfit wyfhod of Arthemesye
Honoured is thurgh al the Barbarye.

O Teuta, queen! thy wyfly chastitee
To alle wyves may a mirour be.
The same thing I seye of Bilia,
Of Rodogone, and eek Valeria.'

Why should I quote more examples, since so many have killed themselves rather than be defiled? I will conclude that it is better for me to kill myself than be defiled in this way. I will be true to Arveragus and rather kill myself in some way as did Demotoin's dear daughter because she would not be defiled.

Oh, Scedasus, it is very sad to read how your dear daughters died, who killed themselves in such a case. As sad as this, or even more, the Theban maiden who killed herself for Nicanor for just the same kind of ill. Another Theban maiden did the same because a Macedonian had raped her. She vindicated her maidenhood with her death. What shall I say of the wife of Niceratus who took her life in such a case? Also how true to Alcibiades was his love who chose to die rather than let his body be unburied. Behold what a wife Alcestis was,' she said, 'and what does Homer say of good Penelope? All Greece knows of her chastity. By Heaven, thus it is written of Laodamia who refused to survive Protesilaus when he was slain at Troy. I can relate the same of noble Portia, she could not live without her Brutus, to whom she had given her whole heart. The perfect wifehood of Artemisia is honoured throughout barbarian lands. Oh, Queen Teuta, may thy wifely chastity be held up as a mirror for all wives. I say the same of Bilia, Rhodogune, and also Valerie.'

Thus pleyned Dorigene a day or tweye,
Purposinge ever that she wolde deye.   730

But nathelees, upon the thridde night,
Hom cam Arveragus, this worthy knight,
And asked hir, why that she weep so sore?
And she gan wepen ever lenger the more.

'Allas!' quod she, 'that ever was I born!
Thus have I seyd,' quod she, 'thus have I sworn' –
And told him al as ye han herd bifore;
It nedeth nat reherce it yow na-more.

This housbond with glad chere, in freendly wyse,
Answerde and seyde as I shal yow devyse: 740

'Is ther oght elles, Dorigen, but this?'
   'Nay, nay,' quod she, 'god help me so, as wis;
This is to muche, and it were goddes wille.'
   'Ye, wyf,' quod he, 'lat slepen that is stille;
It may be wel, paraventure, yet to-day.
Ye shul your trouthe holden, by my fay!
For god so wisly have mercy on me,
I hadde wel lever y-stiked for to be,
For verray love which that I to yow have,
But-if ye sholde your trouthe kepe and save.   750
Trouthe is the hyeste thing that man may kepe:' –

So for a day or two did Dorigen lament, continually planning to die. But, nevertheless on the third night the worthy knight Arveragus came home and asked her why she wept so bitterly. She wept more and more.

'Alas!' she said, 'that I was ever born. I have said this – I have promised this . . .' and she told him all that you have heard before. There is no need to repeat it again. With cheerful countenance and in a friendly fashion the husband answered and spoke as I shall tell you.

'Dorigen, is there nothing else but this?'

'No!, No!' she replied. 'May God help me indeed, even if it were God's will it is too much.'

'Well, wife,' he said, 'let things that are still sleep on. All could be well perhaps. This very day, by my faith, you must keep your word. For, as sure as God has mercy on me, I would rather be stabbed for the true love I have for you if you do not keep and preserve your word. Truth is the finest thing a man can keep.'

But with that word he brast anon to wepe,
And seyde, 'I yow forbede, up peyne of deeth,
That never, whyl thee lasteth lyf ne breeth,
To no wight tel thou of this aventure.
As I may best, I wol my wo endure,
Ne make no contenance of hevinesse,
That folk of yow may demen harm or gesse.'

And forth he cleped a squyer and a mayde:
'Goth forth anon with Dorigen,' he sayde,   760
'And bringeth hir to swich a place anon.'
They take hir leve, and on hir wey they gon;
But they ne wiste why she thider wente.
He nolde no wight tellen his entente.

Paraventure an heep of yow, y-wis,
Wol holden him a lewed man in this,
That he wol putte his wyf in jupartye;
Herkneth the tale, er ye up-on hir crye.
She may have bettre fortune than yow semeth;
And whan that ye han herd the tale, demeth.   770

This squyer, which that highte Aurelius,
On Dorigen that was so amorous,
Of aventure happed hir to mete
Amidde the toun, right in the quikkest strete,
As she was boun to goon the wey forthright
Toward the gardin ther-as she had hight.
And he was to the gardinward also;
For wel he spyed, whan she wolde go
Out of hir hous to any maner place.
But thus they mette, of aventure or grace;   780
And he saleweth hir with glad entente,
And asked of hir whiderward she wente?

And she answerde, half as she were mad,
'Un-to the gardin, as myn housbond bad,
My trouthe for to holde, allas! allas!'

But with these words he burst into tears and said, 'I forbid you, on pain of death, ever whilst you live or breathe to tell anyone of this adventure – I will endure my sorrow as best I may – nor appear with heavy countenance so that people will guess or think ill of you.'

At once he called a squire and a maidservant.

'Set out with Dorigen immediately,' he said, 'and take her at once where she wishes to go.'

They take their leave and go on their way, but they know not the reason she went there. He would not tell anyone of his purpose.

Perhaps a number of you indeed will think him a foolish man because he put his wife in jeopardy. Listen to the tale before you cry out against him. She may well have better fortune than it appears to you now. Decide when you have heard the story.

By chance the squire called Aurelius, who loved Dorigen so much, happened to meet her just in the centre of the town, in the busiest street, as she prepared to make her way straight to the garden where she had given her promise. He was also on his way there, for he kept watch to see when she would leave her house to go anywhere. So they met, by chance or the grace of God. He greeted her with happy attention and asked her whither she was going. As though she were half-mad, she answered, 'To the garden, as my husband ordered me, to keep my promise, alas! alas!'

Aurelius gan wondren on this cas,
And in his herte had greet compassioun
Of hir and of hir lamentacioun,
And of Arveragus, the worthy knight,
That bad hir holden al that she had hight,   790
So looth him was his wyf sholde breke hir trouthe;
And in his herte he caughte of this greet routhe,
Consideringe the beste on every syde,
That fro his lust yet were him lever abyde
Than doon so heigh a cherlish wrecchednesse
Agayns franchyse and alle gentillesse;

For which in fewe wordes seyde he thus:
    'Madame, seyth to your lord Arveragus,
That sith I see his grete gentillesse
To yow, and eek I see wel your distresse,   800
That him were lever han shame (and that were routhe)
Than ye to me sholde breke thus your trouthe,
I have wel lever ever to suffre wo
Than I departe the love bitwix yow two.
I yow relesse, madame, in-to your hond
Quit every surement and every bond,
That ye han maad to me as heer-biforn,
Sith thilke tyme which that ye were born.
My trouthe I plighte, I shal yow never repreve
Of no biheste, and here I take my leve,   810
As of the treweste and the beste wyf
That ever yet I knew in al my lyf.
But every wyf be-war of hir biheste,
On Dorigene remembreth atte leste.
Thus can a squyer doon a gentil dede,
As well as can a knight, with-outen drede.'

Aurelius wondered about this and, in his heart, he had great pity for her and her sorrow, and for the worthy knight Arveragus who had made her carry out all she had promised, so hateful was it to him that his wife should break her word. His heart filled with great pity, seeing the best on every side, that he had rather give up his desire than do such a mean, miserable act contrary to generous and noble feeling.

So briefly he spoke thus: 'Madame, tell your lord Arveragus that since I see his great kindness to you and also see your distress, that he would rather be shamed than you should break your promise, I would much rather suffer agony for ever than come between your love for one another. Madame, I release you from every pledge and bond made by you since the time you were born. I give my word I shall never reproach you for any promise. I take here my leave of the truest and best wife that I ever knew in all my life.'

But let every wife beware of her promises – at least remember Dorigen. So can a squire perform a noble deed, without a doubt as well as a knight.

She thonkëth him up-on hir knees al bare,
And hoom un-to hir housbond is she fare,
And tolde him al as ye han herd me sayd;
And be ye siker, he was so weel apayd,   820
That it were inpossible me to wryte;
What sholde I lenger of this cas endyte?

Arveragus and Dorigene his wyf
In sovereyn blisse leden forth hir lyf.
Never eft ne was ther angre hem bitwene;
He cherisseth hir as though she were a quene;
And she was to him trewe for evermore.
Of thise two folk ye gete of me na-more.

Aurelius, that his cost hath al forlorn,
Curseth the tyme that ever he was born: 830
'Allas,' quod he, 'allas! that I bihighte
Of pured gold a thousand pound of wighte
Un-to this philosophre! how shal I do?
I see na-more but that I am fordo.
Myn heritage moot I nedes selle,
And been a begger; heer may I nat dwelle,
And shamen al my kinrede in this place,
But I of him may gete bettre grace.
But nathelees, I wol of him assaye,
At certeyn dayes, yeer by yeer, to paye,   840
And thanke him of his grete curteisye;
My trouthe wol I kepe, I wol nat lye.'

On her bare knees she thanks him, and goes home to her husband. She told him all that you have heard me say. Be sure that he was so pleased that it is impossible for me to describe. What more of this matter should I recount?

Arveragus and his wife Dorigen lived their lives in the future in supreme bliss. Never after was there any anguish between them. He cherished her as though she were a queen and she was true to him for evermore. You get no more from me about these two.

Aurelius, who had lost all his outlay, cursed the time that he was ever born. 'Alas!' he said, 'alas! that I promised a thousand pounds weight of refined gold to that philosopher. What shall I do? I see nothing more than the fact that I am ruined. I shall have to sell my inheritance and become a beggar. I cannot live here and shame my family unless I can get mercy from him. I will try to pay on fixed dates year by year and thank him for his kindness. I will keep my bond, I will not lie.'

   With herte soor he gooth un-to his cofre,
And broghte gold un-to this philosophre,
The value of fyve hundred pound, I gesse,
And him bisecheth, of his gentillesse,
To graunte him dayes of the remenaunt,
And seyde, 'maister, I dar wel make avaunt,
I failled never of my trouthe as yit;
For sikerly my dette shal be quit   850
Towardes yow, how-ever that I fare
To goon a-begged in my kirtle bare.
But wolde ye vouche-sauf, up-on seurtee,
Two yeer or three for to respyten me,
Than were I wel; for elles moot I selle
Myn heritage; ther is na-more to telle.'

   This philosophre sobrely answerde,
And seyde thus, whan he thise wordes herde:
'Have I nat holden covenant un-to thee?'
'Yes, certes, wel and trewely,' quod he.   860
'Hastow nat had thy lady as thee lyketh?'
'No, no,' quod he, and sorwefully he syketh.
'What was the cause? tel me if thou can.'
Aurelius his tale anon bigan,
And tolde him al, as ye han herd bifore;
It nedeth nat to yow reherce it more.
   He seide, 'Arveragus, of gentillesse,
Had lever dye in sorwe and in distresse
Than that his wyf were of hir trouthe fals.'
The sorwe of Dorigen he tolde him als,   870
How looth hir was to been a wikked wyf,
And that she lever had lost that day hir lyf,
And that hir trouthe she swoor, thurgh innocence:
'She never erst herde speke of apparence;
That made me han of hir so greet pitee.
And right as frely as he sente hir me,
As fely sente I hir to him ageyn.
This al and som, ther is na-more to seyn.'

With a sad heart he went to his coffers and took gold to the philosopher, I should think to the value of five hundred pounds, and begged him in his generosity to grant him time to pay the rest. He said, 'Sir, I can boast I never as yet failed in my bond, and my debt to you shall be repaid for sure, however I may fare myself by going begging in my bare tunic. If you would give me two or three years respite on security then I would be well. Otherwise I must sell my inheritance. There is no more to say.'

When he had heard these words the philosopher answered gravely and spoke thus:

'Have I not kept my covenant with you?'

'Yes, surely, well and truly,' he replied.

'Have you not had your lady as it pleases you?'

'No, no,' he said and sorrowfully sighed.

'What was the reason? Tell me if you can.'

Aurelius at once began his tale and told him all that you have heard before; so there is no need to repeat it any more.

He said: 'Arveragus would in his nobility rather die in sorrow and distress than that his wife should ever be false to her word.' He also told him of Dorigen's grief. How loathsome it was to her to be a wicked woman, and how she would rather have lost her life the day that, in innocence, she gave her promise. She had never before heard tell of illusions. That made me take such great pity on her and, as generously as he sent her to me, I sent her back again to him. That's the sum of it all, there is no more to tell.'

This philosophre answerde, 'leve brother,
Everich of yow dide gentilly til other.   880
Thou art a squyer, and he is a knight;
But god forbede, for his blisful might
But-if a clerk coude doon a gentil dede
As wel as any of yow, it is no drede!
Sire, I relesse thee thy thousand pound,
As thou right now were cropen out of the ground,
Ne never er now ne haddest knowen me.
For sire, I wol nat take a peny of thee.
For al my craft, ne noght for my travaille.
Thou hast y-payed wel for my vitaille;   890
It is y-nogh, and farewel, have good day:'
And took his hors, and forth he gooth his way.
Lordinges, this question wolde I aske now,
Which was the moste free, as thinketh yow?
Now telleth me, er that ye ferther wende.
I can na-more, my tale is at an ende.

Here is ended the Frankeleyns Tale.

The philosopher answered. 'Dear brother, each of you acted nobly towards the other. You are a squire, and he is a knight but, God forbid in his blessed majesty, that a magician could not do a noble deed as well as any of you (of that) there is no doubt.

Sir, I release you from your thousand pounds, as though you had appeared out of the ground for the first time and had never known me before. Sir, I will not take a penny from you either for my skill or my work. You paid me well for the food I gave you. It is enough, farewell and good-day!'

He took his horse and went forth on his way.

Gentlemen, I will now ask you a question. Who does it seem to you was the most generous? Tell me before you go any further. I can say no more, my tale is at an end.

Here ends the Franklin's Tale.

Chaucer's grammar

It should not be forgotten that, in point of time, Chaucer stands midway between King Alfred, who died in 901, and ourselves. We shall therefore expect that the language he wrote will represent a transitional stage between Old English and Modern English, and this is in fact what we find. Old English, sometimes still called Anglo-Saxon, was a fully inflected language, closely resembling Modern German in the variety and complexity of its endings. Modern English has very few inflexions, and those it has are very simple to learn. Chaucer's inflexions are much fewer than King Alfred's were, though more than our own. What we shall see is that a very large number of the inflexions of Old English are represented in Chaucer by the single letter *-e*, which is as a rule pronounced; in Modern English we write the *-e* but do not pronounce it. The details below are not a complete account of Chaucerian inflexion, but will be a guide to much of his grammar and of his versification. Some of the inflexions in Old English were made by changing the root vowels in both nouns and verbs, and these changes are mostly preserved in Chaucer. But even so, as early as the poet's time, there was a tendency to get rid of irregular or anomalous forms, and to require all words to conform to pattern. We shall now indicate the normal structure of Middle English as shown in Chaucer's work; abnormalities will be pointed out in the notes on particular words.

Nouns

There is no standard termination for the nominative and accusative singular. The dative singular ends in *-e*, and all other cases, singular and plural end in *-es*. As sometimes the nominative and accusative also end in -*e*, it must be remembered that a final -*e* is not a sure sign of the dative singular of a noun. Sometimes the -*es* becomes -*s* in a long word.

Some words have plurals in -*en* or -*n*; these are survivals of Old English nouns which had plurals in -*an*; we still have 'oxen' in Modern English, and a few others.

Prepositions all take the dative case.

Adjectives

A few adjectives end normally in -*e* in the nominative and accusative singular, but most end in a consonant. In the plural, all adjectives end in -*e*. But when an adjective is preceded by a demonstrative or a possessive adjective, such as 'the', 'his', 'your', it has an -*e* in all cases, both singular and plural. This form in -*e* is called the 'weak' form: the uninflected singular is called 'strong'.

The comparatives end in -*er* and the superlatives in -*este*. The ancestors of the modern irregular comparisons are, naturally, found in Chaucer.

Pronouns

These are so like the Modern English pronouns that we shall not need to say much about them. We shall not, however, find forms corresponding to our 'its', 'their', and 'them'. Instead we shall find 'his' used for persons and things, 'hir' (which is easily confused with 'hir' which means 'her'), and 'hem' respectively. Sometimes the pronoun 'thou' is attached to the verb when used in an interrogative sentence. We find 'maistow' for 'mayst thou'.

The plural of 'that' is 'tho', not 'those'.

The relatives show the greatest differences from the modern pronouns. Our 'who' is not relative in Chaucer, but interrogative. We find that 'that' is the chief relative if followed

by 'he', 'his', or 'him' after an interval of a few words. 'That
... he' will be translated by 'who'; 'that ... his' by 'whose';
and 'that ... him' by 'whom'. 'Whiche' is used as a relative
in the singular and plural, for persons and things. We may
still say, 'Our Father, Which art in Heaven ...' 'Whos' and
'whom' were used as relatives, although 'who' was not.

'Which?' means 'of what kind?' When 'what' is used in-
terrogatively it means 'why'.

The chief indefinite pronoun is 'man', or 'men'. It is used
like the French *on*, and should as a rule be translated by
'anyone', or 'we'.

Verbs

These are either strong or weak, according to the method of
formation of the past tense and past participle. Change of
vowel characterizes a strong verb: addition of *-ede*, *-de*, or
-te to form past tense, and of *-ed*, *-d*, or *-t* to form past participle indicates a weak verb.

The conjugations of a typical strong and weak verb are as
follows:

			Strong **to** **singen**	Weak **to** **maken**
Indicative	*Singular*	1	singe	make
Present		2	singest	makest
		3	singeth	maketh
	Plural	1, 2, 3	singe(n)	make(n)
Subjunctive	*Singular*	1	singe	make
Present		2	singe	make
		3	singe	make
	Plural	1, 2, 3	singe(n)	make(n)
Indicative	*Singular*	1	song	made
Past		2	songe	madest
		3	songe	made, maked
	Plural	1, 2, 3	songe(n)	made(n), makede(n)

Subjunctive	*Singular*	1 songe	made
Past		2 songe	made
		3 songe	made
	Plural 1, 2, 3	songe(n)	made(n)
Imperative	*Singular*	sing	make
	Plural	singe(th)	make(th)
Participles	*Present*	singinge	makinge
	Past	ysonge(n)	ymaked, maad
Infinitive	*Present*	singe(n)	make(n)

There is a tendency for a final *-n* to drop off.

Adverbs

Many adverbs resemble the weak adjective, having the *-e* ending; others add *-ly* to the adjective. Those in the first group lose their *-e* eventually, and give us in Modern English the phenomenon of adjectives and adverbs of the same form: *e.g.* He runs fast, he is a fast runner.

Chaucer's pronunciation

It would be easier, and more fun, to learn the pronunciation of Chaucer's English by listening to gramophone records of Chaucer's poetry in what is considered to be the original pronunciation. Several recordings have been made of modern scholars reading Chaucer. We particularly recommend the reading of the Prologue to *The Canterbury Tales* (Argo, PLP 1001) mentioned at the end of the Bibliography, p.6. However, it will be helpful to study the following table, which indicates approximately Chaucer's pronunciation:

Vowels
In words of English origin
Short vowels

a pronounced like *a* in French *placer*; but not like *a* in English 'cat'.

e pronounced like *e* in Modern English 'men'.

i pronounced like *i* in 'pin'. *y* is often written for *i* and has the same sound as *i*.

o pronounced like *o* in 'not'. Before letters written with a number of short strokes, like *m*, *n*, and especially a combination of these two, *o* is written for *u*, and should be pronounced like *u*, as for example, in *comen, somer*; (like 'love' or 'monk').

u pronounced like *u* in 'pull', or like *oo* in 'soot'; but not like *u* in 'duke'.

Long Vowels
It is often possible to recognize a long vowel by its being duplicated in writing. For example, *taak* contains a long *ā*; *sooth* contains a long *ō*.

ā pronounced like *a* in 'father'.

ē pronounced either like é (acute) or like è (grave) in French. Only a knowledge of the origin of the words in Old English can guide the reader to distinguish between these close and open sounds, as they are called; but the former sound is usually represented in Modern English by *ee*, and the latter by *ea*. Modern English *need* had a close vowel in Old English, where it was spelt *nēd*; Modern English *mead*, a meadow, was *mēd* in Old English, with an open vowel. As an indication that these two vowels had distinct sounds we may note that Chaucer very rarely makes them rhyme.

ī often written *y*, pronounced like *ee* in 'feel'.

ō pronounced either like *o* in *so*, or like *a* in 'call'. Chaucer recognizes the different pronunciations just as he distinguishes the two long *e* sounds. In Modern English the former sound is represented by *oo*, as in 'soon' while the latter is like the vowel sound in 'note'.

ū pronounced like *oo* in 'soon'.

Diphthongs

ai, ei, ay, and *ey*, generally pronounced like the diphthong in 'day', though some authorities believe they were sounded like *i* in 'line'.

au, aw pronounced like *ou* in 'house'; but before the combination – *ght* like the *o* in 'not'.

eu, ew pronounced like *ew* in 'few'.

oi, oy pronounced like *oy* in 'boy'.

ou, ow pronounced like *u*, or like *au, aw*.

In words of French origin

Such of these words as had already become part and parcel of the everyday English speech of that time would obey the rules for the pronunciation of English vowel sounds; the others would retain the vowels of the French language which were sounded much as they are today.

In unaccented syllables

The final -*e*, so common at the end of a line of verse and elsewhere, is sounded like the second syllable of the word 'china'.

Consonants

The consonants have generally the same pronunciation as they have today, with certain slight modifications. There were no silent consonants, unless perhaps the *g* before an *n* is not sounded.

kn is pronounced as in modern German.

gg like *dge* in Modern English 'ridge'.

ng like *ng* in English 'finger'.

gh as in Modern German, may be palatal or guttural according as to whether it is preceded by a palatal or a guttural vowel.

th initial, is sounded as in 'thin', not as in 'then'.

ch in words of both English and French origin, is pronounced as in Modern English 'choose'.

w before *r* is pronounced like a rapidly sounded *oo*.

h in words of French origin is silent. In words of English origin an initial *h* is sounded, but where the metre demands that a final -*e* should be elided before an *h*, that *h* is silent.

Final -*f* is sounded as -*f* and not as *v*.

Final -*s* is sounded as -*s* and not as *z*.

Chaucer's use of the final -*e*

You will have noticed the great number of words ending in -*e*, which is usually sounded. By this device Chaucer obtains a less rigid line that might otherwise have been the case. As a rule, however, the -*e* at the end of a word is not sounded if the first letter of the following word is a vowel.

The termination is itself what is left, in Middle English, of an inflexion in Older English. In the passage 583 to 594 several words in *-e* represent an Old English termination, and their original functions are as follows:

583 **righte** Vocative case of adjective.
584 **drede** Present indicative of verb.
   love Present indicative.
585 **were** Past subjunctive.
   displese Present infinitive.
586 **nere** Past subjunctive.
   have Present indicative.
   disese Accusative case of noun.
587 **moste** Present tense.
588 **wolde** Past tense.
   telle Present infinitive.
   me Dative of pronoun.
589 **dye** Present infinitive.
   pleyne Present infinitive.
590 **ye** Nominative plural of pronoun.
   slee Present tense.
   peyne Dative case of noun.
591 **routhe** Accusative of noun.
592 **breke** Present tense.
   trouthe Accusative case of noun.
593 **thilke** Adjective.
594 **ye** Pronoun.
   cause Noun of Latin origin.
   love Present subjunctive.

Examples of other endings in *-e* are:

 43 **loke** Plural imperative.
161 **kepe** Imperative singular.
163 **wele** Nominative of a weak adjective.
204 **on-lyve** Adverbial ending.
219 **manye** Plural adjective.
250 **swete** Vocative of adjective.
464 **gretteste** Superlative of adjective.

Chaucer's versification

In earlier poems, Chaucer had used various metres, among which the eight-syllabled line was common. In *The Canterbury Tales*, however, he generally employs ten-syllabled lines, rhyming in couplets and with a break – known as a caesura – after the fifth syllable. But, as a series of lines with a break in the middle of each would be monotonous and irritating and not in keeping with the style of the tales, he varied the position of the caesura. We find examples of this variety of position in the paragraph beginning at line 627. In the first line, the pause comes after the fourth syllable; in 628 and 629 after the fifth; and in 630, 631, and 632 after the fourth again. In 633 the pause appears to come after the second syllable, an unusual position; in 634 it follows the sixth. In the next three lines, 635–7, the stress is on the fourth syllable once more, but in 638 it is again on the second.

When counting up the number of syllables in a line, we should remember that the final *-e* of a word does not count if it comes immediately before a vowel, or an *h*, and that the endings *-ioun* and *-ience* are counted as two and three syllables respectively.

The Franklin's Tale consists of 896 lines, the lines rhyming in pairs. So long a poem might easily become unwieldy, and it is interesting to notice a method whereby Chaucer prevents the poem from becoming disjointed. He frequently ends a paragraph, not on the second of two rhyming lines but on the first, and so links the following paragraph to the previous one. Many examples of this device will be found throughout the poem, when the second paragraph introduces a fresh phase of the story: for example, lines 352 and 353; 423 and 424; 527 and 528.

Textual notes

The passage from the Prologue to
The Canterbury Tales, lines 331–60

331 **A Frankelyn** Literally, 'a free man', he was a wealthy
landowner, but not one of the nobility. As his companion on
the road to Canterbury was a Sergeant of the Lawe, we may
assume that he was himself a man of some importance, for it
was from among that small number of legal experts that
Judges of the Common Law were chosen.

333 **complexioun** Temperament.
sangwyn Confident. What we read of him in his talk with
the Squire and in his telling of the story testifies to his self-
confidence.

334 **a sop in wyn** A cake dipped in wine. We read also of his
delight in other good things which might well be found on the
table dormant – or permanent table – which was always
ready in his hall.

335 **liven in delyt** This phrase sums up one side of his character;
but he occupied himself also as a public benefactor in his
neighbourhood, and at Westminster as a Member of
Parliament.

336 **Epicurus** A Greek philosopher of the third century BC,
taught that the highest happiness for a man to desire was to
have his body free from pain, and his mind free from fears.

340 **Seint Julian** The patron saint of the hospitable.

341 **after oon** Up to one standard, and that the highest.

342 **bettre envyned** With a better stock of wine.

343 **bakemete** Fish and meat pies, pasties. Only the rich could
afford either fish or meat.

345 **Snowing** This metaphor suggests the extent of the bounty to
be found in his household, and especially in his hall. It also
emphasizes his wealth and his generosity.

349 **mewe** When the area by the royal palace in London was no
longer required for fattening fowls, it was given over to

stabling for horses. Hence the later use of the word 'mews' generally.

350 **breem** A freshwater fish.

luce The voracious fish, usually called the pike.

stewe A pond in which fish were kept until wanted for the table.

353 **table dormant** Permanent table, as distinguished from one which would be brought into use for mealtimes only.

354 **covered** Set for a meal (the plate, knife, fork, spoon etc., were still referred to as 'covers' in the novels of Dickens and Thackeray).

355 **lord and sire** President.

356 **knight of the shire** Member of Parliament for a county.

The words of the Franklin to the Squire and of the Host to the Franklin

1 **Squier** A squire ranked next below a knight in order of chivalry. This Squire was the Knight's son. His tale was never finished. In *Il Penseroso*, Milton asks the Goddess of Melancholy to

'Call up him that left untold,
The story of Cambuscan bold
Of Camball, and of Algarsife,
And who had Canace to wife,
That owned the virtuous ring and glass,
And of the wondrous horse of brass
On which the Tartar king did ride.'

The reference is clearly to Chaucer and the *Squire's Tale*.

thee wel y-quit You have done very well. The Squire had not finished his tale when the Franklin spoke to him: indeed the tale was never completed.

2 **gentilly** Freely, sincerely.

3 **thy youthe** *The General Prologue* says that he was 'of twenty yeer of age'. Notice that Chaucer lets 'allow the' in line 4 to rhyme with 'thy youthe' in this line.

5 **as to my doom** In my judgement.
11 **twenty pound worth lond** Land with a rental value of twenty pounds a year.
12 **right now** This very minute.
13 **were** Subjunctive mood, governed by the word 'lever' in line 11.
   discrecioun Sense of values.
14 **fy on possessioun** What is the real value of property if a man is not worthy in himself. The Franklin's son had evidently plenty of money but wasted it in dicing.
16 **and yet shal** And shall do it again.
20 **hath lever** Prefers.
   talken Chatter.
21 **comune** Have serious conversation.
   gentil Well-bred.
22 **gentillesse** Manners suitable to a young fellow of his station in life.
23 **straw for your gentillesse** Harry Bailly, the Host, who has no opinion of the good breeding which the Franklin, a man of some standing, would value pooh-poohs the talk he has overheard about good manners, and reminds the Franklin that, according to the luck of the draw they had made at the beginning of the pilgrimage, it is his turn to tell a tale to beguile the tediousness of the journey to Canterbury.
26 **atte leste a tale or two** Chaucer's programme could hardly have been carried out: twenty-nine stories would have had to be provided if each had told only one tale. Actually only twenty-four tales were told and of these four are incomplete.
27 **haveth me nat in desdeyn** Do not be offended with me.
30 **withouten wordes mo** Without any more talk.
34 **as fer as** So long as my wits do not play me false.
35 **that it may plesen yow** The Host was to decide who had told the best story, the prize being a dinner at the Tabard, paid for by all the other competitors. This reference to the Host's taste in literature can hardly be taken seriously.

The Franklin's Prologue

37 **thise** Those.
   gentil Noble, worthy.
38 **aventures** Happenings, adventures.
   layes Short poems, embodying narratives.
39 **hir firste** Their original.
41 **redden** Read silently.
42 **oon of hem** It is not yet possible to say which lay, if any, was
   the original of *The Franklin's Tale*. Possibly Chaucer invented
   it.
43 **as I can** To the best of my ability.
44 **sires** Note that throughout his tale, the Franklin never
   addresses himself to the ladies in the party of pilgrims.
   burel Plain, unlearned, uncultured. The tale, however, does
   not support the plea of boorishness.
46 **excused of** Pardoned for.
47 **rethorik** The art of public speaking.
49 **Mount of Pernaso** Mount Parnassus. It was here that the
   Nine Muses, who inspired poets and other singers during
   sleep, were said to live.
50 **Cithero** Cicero, whose speeches had long been held to be
   models of oratory. He died in 43 BC.
51 **colours** Ornaments of style.
52, 53 Here the Franklin refers in a play upon words to the actual
   colours of flowers in the fields the Pilgrims may be passing at
   the time.
54 **colours of rhetoric** Fine phrases of oratory.
   to queynte Too difficult.
55 **feleth noght of** Is not moved by at all.
56 **yow list** It pleases you.

The Franklin's Tale

1 **Armorik** Is said to have received its present name of
   Britanny when a number of Christians, expelled from Britain,
   settled there in the fifth century. It was known to the Romans
   as Armorica.
2 **dide his payne** Did his utmost, his level best.

6 **oon, the faireste** One of the most beautiful.
. **under sonne** On earth.
7 **come** Descended.
8 **wel unnethes** With the greatest difficulty.
for drede For very fear.
9 **peyne** Anguish, torment.
10 **atte laste** Eventually, at the last, in the end.
12 **swich a pitee caught** Conceived such pity.
penaunce Distress.
13 **fil of his accord** Consented to his suit, fell into agreement
with him.
15 **swich lordshipe** Kind of authority.
17 **as a knight** As a knight should, on his word as a knight.
19 **take no maistrie** Take no authority upon himself.
20 **kythe hir jalousie** Show jealousy of her.
22 **shal** Should show to his lady.
23 Except that he would retain the name – though not the reality
– of lordship, lest he should bring discredit upon his rank as a
knight, or husband.
27 **so large a reyne** So wide a kingdom.
28 **ne wolde never god** May God never will.
30 **as in my gilt** For which I was responsible.
31 **have heer my trouthe** Accept my promise.

33–58 Here the Franklin is indulging in a digression, the subject of
which is the conditions whereby a husband and wife may live
a happy married life. It is addressed primarily to the men of
the party.

35 **holden companye** Preserve their companionship.
40 **of kinde** By their very nature.
43 **loke** Look, consider.
who that The man who, whoever.
44 **al above** Above all others.
46 **thise clerkes** Learned men.
47 **sholde never atteyne** Would never succeed in
accomplishing.
49 **so moot I goon** I promise you, I can tell you.

50 'You will have to learn it, whether you will or no.'

52 **that he ne dooth** Who does not do.

53 **constellacioun** Influence of the planets.

55 **complexioun** Temperament: it was believed that a person's temperament was controlled by the planets.

57 **after the tyme** According to circumstances.
temperaunce Restraint.
can on Knows about, practises.

59 The Franklin returns to the narrative.

60 'Promised her every consideration.'

61 **gan to swere** Swore. Here as elsewhere the phrase 'gan to' is used to introduce a past tense (but see line 734).

62 **defaute in here** This means 'failure on her part'. This is an important line: the turning point of the story is the risk of a certain 'failure' on the part of Dorigen, and how she had wit enough to avoid it.

63 **may men seen** We may see. ('Men' is an indefinite article, as in line 48.)

64 The husband is her servant, because he loves his wife, and her lord because he is the man.

73 **Penmark** Scholars agree that by 'Penmark' Chaucer is referring to a place not far from Brest on the rocky coast of Britanny. It is now called 'Penmarc'h'.

79 **which** Used in Middle English where we should use 'who'. The opening words of the Lord's Prayer in the Authorized Version of the Bible retain this use.

80 **'Who was known as Arveragus of Kayrrud.'** It has been suggested that Kayrrud may mean 'the red house' or 'the red town'. In his verse translation of *The Canterbury Tales*, Professor Coghill adopts the spelling 'caer-rhud'.

84 **lust** This word exemplifies how words deteriorate in meaning. In Chaucer's time it meant *pleasure, wholesome desire*.

85 The main events of the tale take place during the stay of Arveragus in England. It is not known to what book the Franklin is referring as his source-book for the tale.
yeer In earlier English the word had no inflexion for the plural, we still speak of 'a ten-year old'.

86 **this Arveragus** Our hero Arveragus. In modern English the

word 'this' is sometimes used to imply a sense of
disparagement or contempt. In Chaucer's day no such
suggestion arises. A similar use of the word is to be seen in line
90, but reinforced with the word 'noble'.

90 **hem lyketh** It pleases them.

94 **whiche that** Who.

95 **in al that ever they may** In every way they can think of.

99 **with al hir bisinesse** As attentively as they can.

101 **by proces** In process of time.

102 **men may** We may. The word 'men' is used much as is the
French pronoun 'on'.
graven on a stone Engrave on a precious stone.

103 **figure** Definite impression.
ther-inne Thereon.

106 **th' emprenting** The imprint, mark, effect.
consolacioun Comforting.

107 **gan aswage** Grew less. The verb **gan** is the past tense of
ginnan, to begin. It is also, as here, used as an auxillary verb
to form the past tense, followed by an infinitive.

108 **rage** Violent grief.

109 **in al this care** In the midst of all this distress.

111 **hastily again** Back again quickly.

113 **gan to slake** Began to grow less violent.

115 **romen hir in companye** Stroll in (their) company.

117 **graunted that requeste** Agreed to that wish of theirs.

122 **where-as** From which.

123 **where-as** Whither.

124 **a parcel of hir wo** Part and parcel of his distress.

126 **of so manye as I see** Out of the number I see.

127 'Freed from the sting of its bitter sufferings.'

131 Here we have the first reference to the black rocks, and their
effect upon her. Her lament prepares us for her rash promise
to Aurelius, lines 261–70.

136 **colde** Baneful. We have a similar use of 'cold' in the phrase
'a cold stare'.

139 **in ydel** Without a definite purpose.
as men seyn As we say.

141–2 **foul confusion** Wicked misuse of work.

142 **fair creacioun** Gracious or worthy creation.

144 **unresonable** Not characteristic of a wise creator.

147 **to my wit** As far as I can see.

150 **al be they nat in minde** Though they are lost to memory, quite forgotten.

151 **which mankinde** And this race of men.

152 **thyn owene merk** Thine own likeness.

160 Dorigen was thinking of the dangers Arveragus might have to encounter.

161 **as kepe my lord** Protect Arveragus.

165 'These rocks stab at my heart for fear of what they may do to him.' This is a third reference to her love for her husband.

172 **ches** Chess was certainly played in the sixth century AD, in India and Persia. The board and the men are traditional. It has been played in England since about the time of the Norman Conquest.

    tables Now known as backgammon, was played in England among the upper classes long before Chaucer's time.

174 **un-to a gardin** The story-teller is preparing us for the meeting with Aurelius.

177 **pleye hem** Amuse themselves.

    al the longe day All the day long.

178–89 **This garden** In his anthology, *The Spirit of Man*, Dr Robert Bridges, once Poet Laureate, quotes these lines for very delight of Chaucer's account of this garden.

184 **the verray paradys** Paradise itself.

186 **lighte** Rejoice.

187 **to gret siknesse** Too severe illness.

190 **at-after diner** After dinner.

192 **which** See note to line 79.

196 **lete her sorwe slyde** Put her sorrow behind her for the time being, though she did not take part in the dance.

197 **up-on** During.

197 **amonges othere men** Most likely Dorigen had not noticed *him* particularly: Dorigen was not herself taking part in the dance; but he had noticed her for 'two yeer and more'.

198 **squyer** The eldest son of a knight was a squire by right of birth. After a severe training in courtly manners in a noble

household, he would become an attendant on his master
during a campaign, in order to complete his probation. The
Franklin had been talking with a squire when the Host called
on him to tell his tale. Chaucer himself had been a squire in
the household of Lionel, Duke of Clarence.

biforen In the sight of.

199 **jolyer of array** More handsomely dressed.

200 **as to my doom** In my opinion.

202 The Franklin almost excels himself in praise of this Squire,
who is to play a chief part in the story.

203 **men sholde** We should.

204 **best faringe** Most handsome.

206 **holden in gret prys** Very highly thought of.

208 **unwiting of this Dorigen at al** Dorigen being quite
unaware of this.

209 **servant to Venus** Venus was the Goddess of Love and
Courtship.

214 The meaning of this line is not clear. It seems, however, to
suggest that he drank all his cup of suffering to the dregs.

217 A general lament, characteristic of lovers who dare not reveal
their love of one lady above others.

219–20 **layes** Short songs.

compleintes Love lyrics.

roundels Songs with a frequently recurring refrain.

virelay Songs with a special rhyme-scheme (a sort of
rondeau).

222 **furie** An avenging or torturing spirit.

223–4 **Echo and Narcisus** Their love has been the subject of
many a poem. Echo, a mountain nymph, had been cursed by
Juno for talking too much. Her punishment was that she
could not begin a conversation but was compelled to repeat
the last words she had heard spoken by others. She fell in love
with Narcissus who himself fell in love with his own reflection
in a fountain; but failing to get into touch with what he
supposed was a beautiful nymph, died of despair.

226 **biwreye** Reveal, disclose (do not translate by 'betray').

228 **kepen hir observaunces** Do not hide their customary
attentions.

230 **as man that asketh grace** As one who appeals for a favour, or mercy.

233 **hir neighebour** Living near her.

234 **worship and honour** High renown and reputation.

235 **tyme yore** For a long time.

236 **fille in speche** Began to talk to one another.

238 **saugh his tyme** Saw his opportunity.

240 'If I was sure it would make your heart glad.'

241 **I wolde** I should wish.

243 'Had gone where I should never have returned from.'

244 **in vayn** To no purpose, fruitless.

245 'My reward is but the bursting of my heart.'

246 **reweth** Have pity. The verb form is imperative.

248 **god wolde** Would to God.
 grave Buried.

250 **do me deye** Make me die: be my death.

251 **gan to loke** Looked (not 'began to look').

253 **never ... ne wiste** Never did I know. A double, emphatic negative.

258 **I wol ben his** Refer to lines 61 and 62.

259 **as of me** So far as I am concerned.

260–70 Dorigen spoke in jest, but Aurelius took her remark in earnest (see lines 271 and 281–2).

264 **what day that** Whenever, on what day.

266 'So that they do not prevent ship or boat from passing.'

270 **in al that ever I can** To the utmost that is possible.

273 'It will never happen.' Dorigen spoke too soon.

277 **whan ... lyketh** Whenever it pleases him.

278 **ful ofte** Again and again.

279 **grief was to Aurelius** i.e. he was sorely grieved.

281 **this were** This would be.

282 A sudden horrible death.

289 **refy the sonne his light** Deprived the sun of its light.

290 An aside from the Franklin, poking fun at the precise terms of the scientists.

295 **him semed** It seemed to him.
 colde Grow cold, chill.

296 **gan holde** Held.

297 **sette him doun** Set himself down, i.e. knelt.

298 **seyde his orisoun** Uttered this prayer. He asked help from
Apollo, begging him with the aid of his sister, the moon, to
perform a miracle which should win Dorigen for him. His
prayer ended with his collapse as recorded in line 352.

299 **verray wo** Sheer grief.

   out of his wit he breyde He took leave of his senses.

300 **niste** (= ne wiste): knew not.

302 **goddes** Gods, not goddess.

305 **after thy declinacioun** Declination. The angular distance
of a heavenly body from the celestial equator. From this point
in the poem we shall come across references to the Aristotelian
scheme of astronomy which considered the earth to be at the
centre of the universe, and the other planets placed each in a
hollow concentric sphere of its own. The eighth sphere
contained the stars, while a ninth sphere surrounded the
whole universe. The earth remained stationary, while the
other planets revolved round it, each at a different rate. (This
account of the solar system is grossly over-simplified, but will
serve the purposes of this edition of the tale.)

307 **herberwe** Position in the heavens.

308 **Phebus** The Sun-god. It is another name for Apollo.

309 **which that am but lorn** Who is entirely lost.

311 **withoute gilt** Who am quite innocent.

312 **dedly herte** Mortal wound.

313 **if yow lest** If it pleases you.

314 **save my lady** With the exception of my lady.

315 'Permit me to tell you clearly.'

317 **Lucina** The moon, which follows the sun to be made alive
by its heat. The sea obeys her and follows her, for she is
goddess of the seas and rivers.

326 **more and lesse** Great and small, in reference to tides.

328 **do myn herte breste** Make my heart break.

329 **opposicioun** Planets are said to be in opposition when they
are directly opposite to one another; in other words, when
they are 180 degrees apart.

330 **Leoun** The sign of the zodiac known as the Lion.
Immediately opposite it is the sign of Aquarius, the Water

Carrier. The point of the prayer of Aurelius is that with the sun in Leo, the Lion, and the moon in Aquarius, the tides would be higher than usual, and hence the rocks would be covered more deeply with water. If then these two heavenly bodies could be kept in the same relative position the rocks could be covered indefinitely, and it might seem that they had actually disappeared, and the terms laid down by Dorigen would seem to have been fulfilled. Aurelius hoped that with the water at depth of five fathoms – thirty feet – the rocks would be sufficiently covered to satisfy Dorigen's conditions.

331 **as preyeth** Pray, entreat.

336 **holdeth your heste** Keep your promise.

337 **dooth** Perform. The verb is imperative.

338 **she** The moon. The notion was that if the sun and moon in conjunction could maintain the pull which would bring such a tide as would cover the rocks for two years, then the conditions imposed by Dorigen would be satisfied.

339 **cours** Journey.

343 **but she vouche-sauf in swiche manere** Unless she promises in the same way.

344–7 **prey to her to sinken** Aurelius has an alternative plan: let the moon sink every rock deep underground into the Kingdom of Pluto, King of the Underworld.

349 If he wins the lady, Aurelius will go on pilgrimage barefoot to the Temple of Phebus in Delphos.

353 **longe tyme** He remained in this state for 'two yeer and more'. See line 374.

358 **chese he, for me** So far as I am concerned he can choose whether to live or die. The comment is the Franklin's.

359–72 By contrast with the sorry plight of Aurelius, we hear of the joy of Arveragus, newly returned from 'Engelond, that cleped was eek Briteyne'. He had gone away again before Aurelius claims Dorigen (line 610).

360 **of chivalreye the flour** This name was later to be given to the Chevalier de Bayard and to Sir Philip Sidney.

366 **no-thing list him** In no way did he desire. 'No-thing' is an adverb.

list him Is pleasing to him.

368 **no doute** No suspicion.

372 In contrast with the happiness of Arveragus, we return to the wretched Aurelius, still 'in langour and in torment', whereas the other was 'in joye and blisse', dancing and making merry.

376 'Before he could walk a foot on the ground.'

377 **which that was a clerk** Who was a scholar.

382 That the Franklin refers to the love of Pamphilus for Galatea suggests that the story would be familiar to his hearers. The brother kept secret the love of Aurelius for Dorigen, although Pamphilus could not keep to himself his own love for Galatea.

383 **with-oute for to sene** Apparently, so far as one would notice.

385 **sursanure** This is a wound apparently healed, although under the surface there is still poisonous matter. The surgeon might perhaps extract the arrow, but there was the risk that he might aggravate the wound and cause further trouble if he was unsuccessful.

387 **come thereby** Get possession of it.

389 **it fell to him in remembraunce** He recalled.

390 It is perhaps a coincidence, and nothing more, that the city of Orleans was in Roman times known as Civitas *Aureliani*. In Chaucer's time it was noted for its faculty of law.

392 **to reden artes** In university parlance today, 'to read' means to study, with a view to an examination in the subject.
curious Profound, abstruse.

395 **he him remembered** He recalled.

396 **studie** Study, library.
he say He saw.

397 **magik naturel** Astrology, that is the influence of the stars and planets, notably the moon.
felawe Fellow student.

399 **al were he** Although he was.

400 **prively** Secretly, not intending that others should see it.

402 **mansiouns** Positions of the moon during the thirty days of a lunar month.

403 **folye** Foolish ideas, rubbish. The Franklin evidently had no admiration for the scientists of his day.

404 'The faith of the Holy Church, as we believe, does not allow any illusion to harm us.'

411 **sciences** Skills.

412 **diverse apparences** Various false appearances, illusions.

413 **thise subtile tregetoures** The clever conjurers we hear about.
    pleye Perform, produce, present.

414 **have I wel herd seye** I have certainly been told.

422 **whan hem lyked** When it pleased them, when they wanted.

425 **old felawe** Former fellow-student.

427 **above** In addition, as well.

428 **sholde wel make** Ought to be able to make.
    his love Dorigen.

429 **with an apparence** With a false show, with some illusion.

432 'And make ships come and go by the cliff and remain in such a fashion for a day or two.'

435 Then must Dorigen keep her 'promise', or else at the very least he shall put her to shame.

446 **which that** Who.

451 **Briton** Breton.

452 The form of the word **'dawes'** – instead of the more usual 'days' – is necessary for the sake of the rhyme.

458 **hem lakked no vitaille** They lacked no kind of food.

459–60 'So well appointed a house as this one was, had Aurelius never seen in all his life.'

461 **he showed him** By some illusion.

462 **wilde deer** Wild animals.

466 'Bled from grievous wounds from arrows.'

467 **voided** Removed.

468 **A fair river** A pleasant hawking ground.

471 'He gave him the great delight of seeing Dorigen taking part in a dance in which he himself was dancing.'

476 **our revel** The Franklin and the others had, as it were, imagined themselves to have seen these marvels.

477 'And yet they did not move out of the house.'

479–80 'But in his study, where his books are, they still are sitting, and no one but these three.'

487 **when it lyketh yow** When it pleases you. (Avoid translating by 'when you like'.)

488 'Though you want it at once.'

489 **as for the beste** As the best thing to do.

490 'Lovers must have rest sometime or other.'

491–2 **fille they in tretee** They got down to discussing what this scholar's reward should be.

494 **Gerounde** The River Gironde.
Sayne The River Seine.

495 **made it straunge** Raised difficulties.
so god him save So may God save his soul.

497 'He would not go into Brittany willingly, even for that amount.'

499 'Your thousand pounds be damned.'

502 **ful drive** Completed.
ben knit Are agreed.

503 **by my trouthe** Upon my honour.

504 'Look now, you are not to keep us here longer than tomorrow through any carelessness or slackness.'

506 **have heer my feith to borwe** Here is my promise as a pledge.

509 **what for his labour** Considering his exertions and his hope of happiness.

510 **of penaunce hadde a lisse** Had some respite from torment.

512 **Britaigne** Brittany.
the righte way The shortest route.

514 **ben descended** Alighted.

515 **as the bokes me remembre** As the books remind me. The Franklin introduces a personal touch here, but it is not known from what source he derived his story. The next eleven lines do not advance the story but seem to be the reminder from the Franklin to his hearers of some of the discomforts of winter.

517 **Phebus** The sun.
wex old Grew old.
hewed lyk latoun Coloured like latoun, a mixed metal like brass or bronze in colour.

518 **declinacioun** See note on line 305. The declination is
greatest in summer and least in winter.
hote Refers to the heat received on earth from the sun,
greatest of course in mid-summer. It is December in Brittany
where Aurelius and his friends have arrived.

521 **I dar wel seyn** I am bold to say.

524 Janus who gives his name to January, is imagined as sitting in
an inn drinking wine from an ox's horn and with a joint of
boar's flesh before him, while jovial fellows raise the shout of
'nowel', a word meaning 'birthday', and shouted, evidently as
an expression of joy, at Christmas time.

525 **bugle-horn** A horn used for drinking and made from the
horn of a bugle, a kind of ox.

526 **tusked swyn** Wild boar.
braun Thick flesh, from the shoulder.

529 **his maister** That is, the 'clerk' in whose house they had
spent a night. We are not told how long the journey from
Orleans had taken them.

530 **doon his diligence** Do his utmost.

538 Another personal comment from the Franklin. It seems,
however, that he uses the terms of astrology correctly.

539 **she** Dorigen.
every wight Everybody.
seye Declare.

540 The rocks had gone from Brittany.

541 **sonken under grounde** If they were no longer to be seen
the conditions laid down by Dorigen would be fulfilled. (See
note on line 268.)

543 The Franklin has a poor opinion of the magician.
japes Trickery.
cursednesse Wickedness.
supersticious Diabolic.

544 **tables Toletanes** Tables of Toledo. The tables were lists of
corrections necessary in order to calculate the motions of the
heavenly bodies as seen from any particular place. The tables
referred to were compiled by order of King Alfonso of Castile
in the thirteenth century and were corrected for the city of
Toledo. They would not therefore be correct for use in

Brittany. The clerk is trading on the ignorance of the two brothers.

547 **collect** Collected in groups. *Calculations*, for extended periods of years, of changes of a planet's position.
expans yeres Refers to calculations for much shorter periods than 'collect' above, with which it contrasts.

548 **rootes** Data.
geeris Tackle.

549 **as been** Such as.
centres Points on the rete of an astrolabe, which was an instrument held in the hand, for observing the positions of the stars. Chaucer had written a treatise on the astrolabe for 'litel Lowis my sone', then not quite ten years old. The 'rete' was an 'open work metal plate affixed to an astrolabe and serving to indicate positions of the principal fixed stars'.
argument Mathematical quantity from which another may be deduced.

550 **proporcionels convenients** Tables of suitable proportional parts.

551 **equacions** Adjustments according to circumstances.

553 **Alnath** The name. Still used, of a star in the constellation of Aries, the Ram.

555 **ninthe speere** This sphere is the farthest from the earth and contains the whole of the universe within itself.

556 This line suggests the Franklin's contempt for the whole proceeding.

557 **mansioun** This is the sign of the zodiac in which a planet is believed to have its greatest influence. The clerk was concerned with the moon, the planet nearest to the earth, and its rising; when he had ascertained the details he required, he could calculate other facts necessary to his operation.

560 **face** The third part of a sign of the zodiac; as there were twelve signs, each would include thirty degrees, and a face would include ten degrees. Unequal divisions were called terms.

564 **illusions** Deceptive appearances.
meschaunces Deception.

566 **for which** For which reason, wherefore.

568 **were aweye** Had disappeared.
569 **which that is** Who is.
  despeired By no means certain.
570 **fare amis** Come off badly.
571 **awaiteth on** Waits anxiously for.
572 **noon obstacle** Nothing to hinder his petition to Dorigen.
574 **his maistres feet** The clerk's feet.
576 **lady myn Venus** Venus is the Goddess of Love.
577 **my cares colde** Baneful distresses, cruel suffering.
578 **holde** Taken his way.
581 **humble chere** Modest bearing.
583 **my righte lady** My own true lady.
584 **drede** Reverence.
585 **lothest** Most in fear.
588 'By no means would I tell you how distressed I am.'
589 'But certainly I must either die or lament.'
590 'You slay me who am guiltless through excess of sorrow.'
591 'Though my death gives you no regret.'
593 'Repent, for the fear of the God above.'
596 **of right** Because I have any right to do so.
579 **but your grace** Because of your favour to me.
600 **your trouthe plighten ye** You made a solemn promise.
603 **the honour of yow** To preserve your word of honour.
606 **vouche-sauf** Condescend to do so.
609 'It rests on you entirely to let me live or die.'
613 She did not imagine she would have fallen into such a trap.
616 'Such an unnatural or marvellous happening.'
623 **out of toune** Out of the town of Kayrrud. (Do not translate
  by 'out of town'.)
627 **on thee, fortune, I pleyne** My lament, fortune, is against
  thee.
628 'Who hast entangled me, unawares, in thy chain.'
631 **bihoveth me** I must.
632 **have I lever lese** I will more readily lose.
633 **have a shame of** Bring shame upon.
635 **I may be quit** I may be freed from knowing myself a
  breaker of my promise, and from losing my good name.
639–728 **thise stories beren witnesse** Here follow brief

references to twenty-two virtuous ladies – wives, widows or unmarried – who rather than lose their chastity, suffered death, often at their own hand. There is no doubt that Chaucer found his examples in a treatise written in Latin by the famous St Jerome, who had translated into Latin the version of the Scriptures known as the Vulgate. In the treatise, known as 'Adversus Jovinianum', he combated the views of Jovinian who had decried the virtue of virginity, and had poured scorn on marriage.

(Students may be assured that it is quite unnecessary for them to commit to memory the names of these virtuous women, or to get by heart the individual good deeds for which Dorigen praises them.)

640 **thirty tyrants** They had seized authority in Athens at the beginning of the fifth century BC.

641 **Phidoun** Phidon.

642 'They gave commands to arrest his daughters.'

651 **Messene** Messina.
lete enquere Caused enquiries and search to be made.

652 **Lacedomie** Lacedaemonia, Sparta.

655 **that she nas slayn** Who was not killed.

659 **Aristoclides** Seized the throne of Oechomenos, in Arcadia, in southern Greece.

660 **Stimphalides** Her name was really Stimphalis.

662 **Dianes temple** Diana was a virgin goddess: no man was allowed to enter her temple.

670 **as it thinketh me** As it seems to me.

671 **Hasdrubal** This was not the famous Hasdrubal, brother of Hannibal, but a king of Carthage who was killed in the third Punic War.

677 **Lucresse** Generally called Lucretia, stabbed herself after being outraged by false Sextus, 'who wrought the deed of shame', as mentioned in Macaulay's *Horatius*.

679 **hir thoughte** It seemed to her.

681 **Milesie** One of the greatest of the Greek cities in Asia Minor, had been destroyed by the Persians in 494 BC. It was sacked again by the Gauls in 276 BC.

686 **Habradate** Or Abradates, was King of the Susi, or Persians.

689 **at the leeste way** Whatever happens, at the very least.

690 **if I may** If I can do anything to prevent it.

691 **what sholde I ... sayn** Why should I relate.

696 Dorigen, however, continues to recall the predicaments which befel other ladies.

698 The daughter of Demotion, hearing of the death of the man she was to marry, slew herself lest she should be forced to marry someone else.

700 These sisters, having been violated, killed one another.
for swich maner cas For a similar reason.

704 **Theban** A native of Thebes, in Greece.
for Nichanore Because of her treatment by Nichanore, an officer of Alexander the Great, in the attack on that city.

705 **swich maner wo** Such kind of distress.

709 Nicerates had been put to death by the tyrants of Athens. His wife killed herself before she could become one of their victims.

712 **to dyen chees** Chose to die. The reference is to his concubine, who risked the wrath and revenge of the tyrants by burying his body.

714 **which a wyf** What a splendid wife.
Alceste She consented to die in order to prolong the life of Admetus, her husband. She was, however, brought back from the other world by Hercules.

715 **Penelope** The wife of Odysseus, who kept at bay a host of wooers, from whom she had promised to marry one when she had finished a winding sheet she was making for her husband's father. By undoing at night the work she had done by day she was able to delay a decision until Odysseus returned after a twenty-years' absence and drove the suitors off. (See Homer's Odyssey.)

717 **Laodomya** Her story is told by Ovid. When her husband had been killed at the Siege of Troy, she persuaded the gods to let him return to her for a few hours, and then followed him to the other world. She is usually called Laodamia.

720 **the death of Portia** The death of the wife of Brutus is

referred to in Shakespeare's *Julius Caesar*. Being anxious about his safety she killed herself by swallowing fire.

723 **Arthemesye** The wife of Mausolus, King of Caria, built for him the famous tomb which has given us the word mausoleum.

Barbarye Heathendom.

725 **Teuta** Little is known about this queen of Illyria – a tract of country on the eastern side of the Adriatic.

727 **Bilia** Was the wife of Duillius, the Roman who defeated the Carthaginian fleet in 260 BC.

728 **Rhodogone** Killed her attendant who was trying to make her marry a second husband, and **Valeria** also refused to marry a second time.

730 **she wolde deye** She would kill herself.

732 The whole aspect changes with the return of her husband, Arveragus.

734 **gan wepen** Wept.

737–8 Two lines of comment from the Franklin to the Pilgrims.

739 **glad chere** Cheerful look.

in freendly wise In a kindly way.

742 **as wis** Indeed.

743 **and it were** If it were.

744 **lat slepen that is stille** Let what is at rest sleep on.

745 'All may be well, perhaps, even today, before the day is over.'

746 **trouthe holden** Keep your promise.

747 'May God indeed have mercy on me.'

748 'I had far rather be stabbed to death.'

750 **kepe and save** Preserve and uphold.

752 **brast anon to wepe** Broke at once into tears.

754 'While life or breath lasts for you.'

756 **As I may best** As best I may.

757–8 'Make no appearance of grief so that people may think or guess any evil of you.'

761 **swich a place** Such-and-such a place.

765 **a heep of you** A number of you. The Franklin is speaking to other pilgrims within earshot. (The whole company can hardly have heard all he was saying.)

768 **upon hir crye** Weep over her fate.

769 **than yow semeth** Than seems to you likely.

771 **this squyer** Not, of course, the same as is mentioned in line 759.

774 **quikkest** Busiest.

775 **boun to goon** In the act of going.

777 **was to the gardinward** Was going towards the garden.

779 **to any maner place** Anywhere at all.

783 **mad** Out of her mind.

785 **my trouthe for to holde** To keep my promise.

786 **gan wondren on this cas** Marvelled at this circumstance.

791 **so looth him was** So hateful to him was it.

792 **caughte of this greet routhe** Conceived great sorrow on this account.

793 'Considering from every point of view what was best to be done.'

794 'That it was better for him to keep from his desire.'

798 **for which** Wherefore.

802 **him were lever han shame** He would rather suffer disgrace.

804 **have wel lever** Have much rather.

805 **departe** Separate, break up.

806 **into your hand** (These words should not be taken literally.)

807 **quit** As though discharged.
   surement Pledge, promise.

808 **heer-biforn** Before this day.

810 **of no biheste** Of any promise.

811 **as of** As though of.

813 **be-war** Take good heed.

814 **on Dorigene remembreth** Let her call Dorigen to mind.

815 **a squyer** Aurelius is so described in line 209.

817 **knees al bare** Her bare knees.

818 **is she fare** Has she gone.

819 **han herd me sayd** Have heard me say. (The grammar of this phrase is not orthodox.)

821 **me to wryte** For me to record. This must be Chaucer's own comment; the Franklin was not asked to write about her return to her husband.

825 **angre** Hurt feeling, rather than anger. Arveragus spoke 'in freendly wyse' to her (line 739).

828 **ye gete** You will hear.

829 'Has lost completely all he had spent.'

831 **bihighte** See line 503.

833 **how shal I do** How shall I manage.

834 'All I can see is that I am ruined.'

838 'Unless I can get better favour from him.'

839 **I wol of him assaye** I will try to get his consent.

842 **my trouthe wol I kepe** The importance of the pledged word is insisted on throughout the tale.

847 **dayes of the remenaunt** Days of grace in which to pay the rest of his debt. He owed the Philosopher one thousand pounds (see line 499).

848 **I dare wel make avaunt** I can safely boast.

851 **however that I fare** Even if I have.

852 **to goon a-begged** To go a-begging. In Old English abstract nouns belonging to certain weak verbs were formed by adding -*aþ* or *oþ*, to the stem of the verb. In Middle English this -*aþ*, or *oþ* appears -*ed*. The prefix *a*- represents the O.E. *on*; *a-begged* is therefore the M.E. form of the O.E. *on beggaþ*, and should be translated by 'a-begging'.

855 **were I wel** All would be well as far as I am concerned.

859 **holden covenant** Kept my part of our agreement.

861 **as thee lyketh** As it pleases you, according to your pleasure.

869 **of hir trouthe fals** Untrue to her promise.

871 **how looth hir was** How hateful it was to her.

878 **this al and som** This is the whole truth.

881 The Squire ranked next below the Knight in degrees of chivalry.

883 'If a scholar may not do a noble deed, forsooth.'

884 **it is no drede** There is no doubt.

886 'As if you had at this moment appeared out of the ground,' i.e. 'as if we have never met before'.

890 **vitaille** Hospitality.

891 **have good day** Good-bye.

894 **moste free** Generous.

    as thinketh yow As it seems to you.

896 **I can na-more** I know no more: my tale is finished.
[Chaucer does not report any comments from the Pilgrims in
reply to the Franklin's question in line 894.]

Words in *The Franklin's Tale* liable to be mistranslated

The words in this list resemble closely words used in modern English, but they must be carefully distinguished from their apparent equivalents. Go over this list frequently, in order not to be caught out in a piece of faulty translation which might have been avoided by a more thorough knowledge of vocabulary. Against each word is printed the number of the line where it first occurs in this text, and each word should be considered in its various contexts.

after	57	bisily	323
agayn	20	bisinesse	99
ago	476	bisyde	174
aleye	285	biwreye	226
an	121	boot	266
anoye	147	borwe	506
arte	392	breste	31
as	161	bresting	245
as	886	bugle	525
as in	29	burned	519
as wis	742	but	75
assaye	839	but	309
avaunt	848	can on	58
aventure	212	care	109
awey	336	certeyn	45
		centre	549
bad	783	chalange	596
bank	121	chees	656
bar	381	chese	358
barge	122	clene	267
berd	524	colde	136
bet	694	collect	547
bigon	588	complayne	263

glade	240		knowe	297
glyde	687		knowe	452
governaunce	58		kythe	20
grace	230			
graunte	262		langour	373
graven	102		lasse	496
greet	25		lay	219
grene	134		lese	632
grevaunce	213		leste	157
greve	406		leste	436
guerdon	245		lete	196
			lette	266
hastily	111		leve	100
heed	554		leve	180
heep	765		leve	611
heet	660		leve	879
heigh	7		lever	632
hele	359		lever	795
herberwe	307		lewed	766
here	62		lighte	186
herte	31		lighte	455
herte	463		lighten	322
hevinesse	100		liste	123
hevy	94		longe	177
hight	595		longen	403
his	128		looth	791
holde	188		love	194
hote	595		lust	84
humblesse	25		lusty	209
hyeste	333		lye	357
			lye	842
imaginatif	366		lyke	90
jolyer	199		maistrye	19
juste	370		maner	702
			mansioun	402
kan	58		matere	219
kinde	40		may	108

men	48	quik	608
mene	155	quiken	322
merk	152	quikkest	774
mone	192	quit	635
mone	426	quod	252
moste	195		
		rage	108
namely	11	rather	669
nas	612	raving	298
noght	369	rede	420
noght	546	reden	392
noon	50	repreve	809
noon	406	resoun	105
noon	654	reyn	522
nothing	218	reyne	27
		right	136
oght	741	right	596
oghte	669	rivere	170
operacioun	401	rote	548
oppresse	683		
ordinaunce	175	say	396
oute	367	science	394
overspringe	332	see	119
owene	152	service	244
		seten	480
parcel	124	sette	84
particuler	394	shal	22
passinge	201	sin	263
payne	2	slow	687
penaunce	12	smerte	128
peyne	9	sodeinly	287
playn	470	speche	236
plesaunce	189	spere	552
pleyne	48	stable	143
plighte	809	stike	748
profre	27	streme	519
prosperitee	71	studie	395
prys	183	subtil	413

swete	250		wan	673
syke	136		war	813
syke	372		wayte	535
			wende	613
tables	172		wende	895
temperaunce	57		what	264
than	166		what	437
thanne	658		what	509
ther	73		wher	570
therby	387		wher-as	74
therto	7		wher-so	50
therwith	203		which	192
thinketh	670		wirkyng	552
thise	140		wis	742
tho	284		wit	147
thoughte	473		withoute	383
thriftily	446		wol	30
til	880		wonder	447
to	187		woot	157
touchinge	402		worship	83
travaille	889		worthinesse	10
trespas	638		worthy	59
tretee	491		wrappe	628
			wrecchednesse	543
undertake	483		wys	63
unresonable	144		wyse	316
up-on	197			
			ydel	139
vayn	244		ye	744
vileinye	676		yë	464
			yfostered	146
wake	91			

General questions

1 Do you consider this tale to be the work of a 'burel' man? Give reasons for your opinion.

2 What do you consider to be the chief characteristic of Arveragus?

3 While he was in England, Arveragus wrote letters to Dorigen. Did she write any to him? Add any necessary explanations to your answer.

4 She enjoyed the company of her friends, but there was one fear which she kept to herself. What was that? What importance has this secret to the tale?

5 With what accomplishments does the Franklin credit Aurelius?

6 When did Aurelius find his opportunity of telling Dorigen of his devotion to her? What traits in her character are revealed in her answer to him?

7 Aurelius clung to the slender hope in the reply Dorigen had màde to him, almost in jest; Dorigen, on the other hand, rejoiced in the prospect of her husband's return. What new element now came into the situation?

8 Point out some of the devices whereby Chaucer reminds us that the story is being told by one of the Pilgrims to the others as they are walking along the way to Canterbury.

9 What is the importance of the following words: 'semed' in line 568, 'knew' in 572, and 'wel I woot' in 610?

10 What proof did Dorigen receive that the rocks had actually gone?

11 What action did Arveragus take when he had heard Dorigen's account of her distress?

12 Who are 'an hepe of yow' in line 765?

13 In line 813 we have a reference to the women who were listening to the story. Is there any other such reference?

14 What is there surprising in finding the word 'wryte' in line 821 and 'endyte' in 822?

15 We find the word 'trouthe' six times between lines 751 and 873. Could the importance of keeping one's plighted word be the 'lesson of the poem'?

16 Make a note of the 'asides' made by the Franklin to the Pilgrims. What do they tell us about the Franklin?

Glossary

Abbreviations used in the Glossary

A.N.	*Anglo-Norman*	L.L.	*Late Latin*
Dan.	*Danish*	M.E.	*Middle English*
Du.	*Dutch*	M.H.G.	*Middle High German*
Ety. dub.	*Etymology doubtful*	O.E.	*Old English*
Gk.	*Greek*	O.F.	*Old French*
Icel.	*Icelandic*	O.H.G.	*Old High German*
Lat.	*Latin*	O.N.	*Old Norse*

The meaning of other abbreviations used is obvious; e.g. pres. *for Present Tense*; p.p. *for Past Participle*; p.t. *for Past Tense*.

N.B.—(1) Chaucer used *i* and *y* as equivalents; *ou* and *ow* are interchangeable; so are *-ey-*, *-ay-*, which may be found written *-ei-*, or *-ai-*.

(2) Consult the Notes in association with the Glossary.

Lines from the General Prologue (331–60)

after prep., according to, 347, [O.E. *æfter*].
ale n., ale, 341 [O.E. *ealu*].
alle adj., all, 346 [O.E. *ealle*].
alway adv., always, continually, 353 [O.E. *eal + weg*].
alwey adv., always, continually, 341 [O.E. *eal + weg*].
anlass n., two-edged knife, dagger, [Ety. dub.].

bakemete n., pies, pastry, 343 [O.E. *bacen-mete*].
berd n., beard, 332 [O.E. *berd*].
bettre adv., *better*, 342 [O.E. *betera*].
breed n., bread, 341 [O.E. *brēad*].
breem n., bream, 350 [O.F. *breame*].
but-if conj., unless, 351 [O.E. *būtan + gif*].

chaunge v., change, vary, 348 [O.F. *changer*].

companye n., company, 331 [O.F. *compaignie*].

complexioun n., temperament, 333 [Lat. *complexionem*].

contree n., district, neighbourhood, 340 [O.F. *contre*].

cook n., cook, 351 [O.F. *cōc*].

coude v., knew, 346 [O.E. *coude*].

countour n., auditor of accounts, 359 [O.F. *countour*].

cover v., set for a meal, 354 [O.F. *couvrir*].

dayesye n., daisy, 332 [O.E. *dæges + ēage*].

delyt n., delight, pleasure, enjoyment, 335 [O.F. *delit*].

deyntee n., rarity, delicacy, 346 [O.F. *daintie*].

dormant adj., fixed, permanent, 353 [O.F. *dormir*].

drinke n., drink, 345 [O.E. *drinc*].

envyned v., supplied with wine, 342 [O.F. *enviné*].

felicitee n., happiness, 338 [O.F. *felicité*].

fissh n., fish, 344 [O.E. *fisc*].

flessh n., flesh meat, 344 [O.E. *flæsc*].

ful adv., very, 349 [O.E. *ful*].

gere n., utensils, 352 [O.E. *gere*].

gipser n., pouch, bag, 357 [O.F. *gibicier*].

girdel n., belt, girdle, 358 [O.E. *gyrdel*].

greet adj., great, important, 359 [O.E. *great*].

hadde v., had, 349 [O.E. *hæfde*].

halle n., dining hall, 355 [O.E. *heall*].

hange v., hang [O.E. *hangen*].

heeld v., held; p.t. **holden**, 337.

heeng v., hung; p.t. **hange**, 358.

holden v., hold [O.E. *healden*].

hous n., house, mansion, 343 [O.E. *hūs*].

housholdere n., head of a household, 339 [O.E. *hūs + heald + ere*].

knight n., knight, 356 [O.E. *cniht*].

liven v., live, 335 [O.E. *libban*].

longe adj., long, 354 [O.E. *long*].

lord n., lord, master, president, 355 [O.E. *hlāford*].

luce n., pike – the fish, 350 [O.F. *luce*].

mete n., food, meat, diet, 348 [O.E. *mete*].

mewe v., coop for fattening fowls, 349 [O.F. *mue*].

morne n., morning, 358 [O.E. *morgen*].

morwe n., morning, 334 [O.E. *morgen*].

never adv., never, 343 [O.E. *næfre*].

noon n., no one, none, 342 [O.E. *nān*].

nowher adv., nowhere, anywhere, 342 [O.E. *nāhwǣr*].

oftetyme adv., often, 356 [O.E. *oft + tīma*].

oon adj., one, 341 [O.E. *ān*].

opinioun n., opinion, belief, 337 [O.F. *opinion*].

owne adj., own, very, genuine, 336 [O.E. *āgen*].

parfyt adj., perfect, 338 [O.E. *parfit*].

partrich n., partridge, 349 [O.F. *perdriz*].

plentevous adj., plentiful, 344 [O.F. *plentivous*].

pleyn adj., perfect, complete, 337 [O.F. *plain*].

poynaunt adj., highly flavoured, appetising, piquant, 352 [O.F. *poignant*].

redy adj., ready, 352 [O.E. *rǣde*].

sangwyn adj., confident, 333 [O.F. *sanguine*].

sauce n., sauce, 351 [Lat. *salsam*].

seson n., season, 347 [O.F. *saison*].

sessioun n., session of a law court, 355 [O.F. *session*].

sharp adj., pungent, 352 [O.E. *scearp*].

shire n., shire, county, 356 [O.E. *scīr*].

shirreve n., sheriff, 359 [O.E. *scir + gerēfa*].

sire n., master, 355 [O.F. *sire*].

snewen v., snow, 345 [O.E. *snīwan*].

sondry adj., various, different, 347 [O.E. *syndrig*].

sone n., son, follower, 336 [O.E. *sunu*].

sop n., bread soaked in wine, 334 [O.E. *sopa*].
soper n., supper, 348 [O.F. *soper*].
stewe n., fishpond, 350 [O.F. *estui*].
stood v., remained (p.t. **standen**), 354 [O.F. *standan*].

table n., table, 353 [O.F. *table*].
ther adv., there, 355 [O.E. *þ̄er*].
thinke n., think of, imagine, 346 [O.E. *þincan*].

vavasour n., landholder below the rank of baron, 360 [O.F. *vavassour*].
verraily adv., truly indeed, 338 [O.F. *verrai* + O.E. *līc*].

whit adj., white, 332 [O.E. *hwīt*].
withoute prep., without, 343 [O.E. *wiðūtan*].
wo adj., in trouble, unhappy, 351 [O.E. *wā*].
wone n., habit, custom, 335 [O.E. *wuna*].
worthy adj., distinguished, 360 [O.E. *weorþig*].
wyn n., wine, 334 [O.E. *wīn*].

yeer n., year, 347 [O.E. *gēar*].

The Words of the Franklin to the Squire, and of the host to the Franklin

allow v., applaud, praise, commend, congratulate, 4 [O.F. *allouer*].
atte prep., at the, 25 [O.E. *æt* + *ǣm*].
aright adv., aright, properly, 22 [O.E. *on* + *riht*].

been v., are, 14 [O.E. *bēn*].
biheste n., promise, 26 [O.E. *behæst*].
breken v., break, 26 [O.E. *brecan*].
but-if conj., unless, 15 [O.E. *būton* + *if*].

chaunce n., luck, fortune, 7 [O.F. *cheance*].
comune v., converse, talk seriously, 21 [O.F. *commun*].
consider v., consider, 3 [Lat. *considero*].

continuance n., continuance, 8 [O.F. *continuance*].
contrarien v., oppose your will, 33 [O.F. *contrarier*].

dees n., dice, 18 [O.F. *dez*].
desdeyn n., contempt, 28 [O.F. *desdeign*].
despende v., spend wastefully, 18 [O.F. *despenser*].
deyntee n., pleasure, appreciation, opinion, 9 [O.F. *daintee*].
discrecioun n., discrimination, prudence, 13 [Lat. *discretionem*].
doom n., judgement, opinion, 5 [O.E. *dōm*].

eche pron., each, 25 [O.E. *ælc*].
eloquence n., eloquence, fine speaking, 6 [Lat. *eloquentia*].
entende v., attend, pay heed, 17 [O.F. *entendre*].

fallen v., fall, 12 [O.E. *feallan*].
feelingly adv., tenderly, full of kindly feeling, 4 [O.E. *fēling + līc*].
feith n., faith, 1 [O.F. *fei*].
fer adv., far 34 [O.E. *feorr*].
fy interj., fie! 14 [O.F. *fi*].

gentil adj., well-bred, 21 [O.F. *gentil*].
gentillesse n., good breeding, 22 [O.F. *gentillesse*].
gentilly adv., with all courtesy, worthily, lightly,
  2 [O.F. *gentil* + O.E. *līc*].
gladly adv., readily, 31 [O.E. *glædīce*].

have v., have, hold, 28 [O.E. *habban*].
herkne v., listen to, harken, 32 [O.E. *hercnian*].
hond n., hand, possession, 12 [O.E. *hond*].
host n., host, 31 [O.F. *hoste*].

lerne n., learn, 22 [O.E. *leornian*].
lese v., lose, 19 [O.E. *lēosan*].
leste n., least, 25 [O.E. *lǣst*].
lever adv., rather, sooner, 11 [O.E. *lēofra*].
liste v., wish, desire, 17 [O.E. *lystan*].
lond n., land, 11 [O.E. *lond*].

mo adv., more 30 [O.E. *mā*].
mot v., must, has to, 25 [O.E. *mōt*].
myn adj., my, [O.E. *mīn*].

nat adv., not, 33 [O.E. *nāht*].
non pron., nobody, 5 [O.E. *nān*].

obeye v., obey, 31 [O.F. *obier*].

page n., page, attendant, servant, 20 [O.F. *page*].
pardee interj., by heaven, 24 [O.F. *par + dieu*].
pere n., equal, 6 [O.F. *pair*].
plesen v., please, 35 [O.F. *plaisir*].
pleye v., play, 18 [O.E. *plegian*].
possession n., possession, riches, 14 [O.F. *possession*].
preise v., praise, 2 [O.F. *preiser*].
prey v., pray, beg, 28 [O.F. *preier*].

quod v., said, quoth, 3 [O.E. *cweðan*].

right adv., even, just, 12 [O.E. *rihte*].

sende v., send, 8 [O.E. *sendan*].
seye v., say, 32 [O.E. *secgan*].
sir n., sir, 4 [O.F. *sīre*].
snibbe v., reprove, 16, [O.N. *snubba*].
sone n., son, 10 [O.E. *sunu*].
speche n., speech, 9 [O.E. *spǣc*].
speke v., speak, 4 [O.E. *specan*].
squier n., squire, 1 [O.F. *esquier*].
straw n., straw, rubbish! 23 [O.E. *strēaw*].
suffyse v., prove sufficient, 34 [O.F. *suffise*].
swich adj., such, 13 [O.E. *swylc*].

talken v., talk, chatter, 20 [O.E. *talian*].
tellen v., tell, relate, 25 [O.E. *tellan*].
thee pron., thou, thee, thyself, 1 [O.E. *ðe*].
ther adv., there, where, 5, 22 [O.E. *ðǣ*

thou pron., thou, 1 [O.E. ðu].
though prep., although, 29 [O.E.].
Trinitee n., Trinity, 10 [Lat. *Trinitatem*].

usage n., custom, 19 [O.F. *usage*].

vertu n., valour, worthy pursuits, 8 [O.F. *vertu*].
vertuous adj., worthy, capable, 15 [Lat. *vertuosum*].

wel adv., well, 1 [O.E. *wel*].
what interj., what! now then! 24 [O.E. *hwæt*].
wight n., person, 21 [O.E. *wiht*].
wit n., intelligence, 2 [O.E. *witt*].
with-al adv., likewise, moreover, 15 [O.E. *wiþ + al*].
withouten prep., without, 30 [O.E. *wiþūtan*].
wittes n., wits, intelligence, 34 [O.E. *wittes*].
wol v., will, 31 [O.E. *wol*].
woot v., know, 36 [O.E. *wāt*].
word n., word, 29 [O.E. *word*].
worth n., worth, value, 21 [O.E. *wyrþ*].
wost v., knowest, 24 [O.E. *wast*].
wyse n., way, manner, 33 [O.E. *wīse*].

ye pron., ye, you, 14 [O.E.*gē*].
yet adv., still, again, 16 [O.E. *giet*].
yeve v., give, 7 [O.E. *giefan*].
y-know adv., enough, 36 [O.E. *genōh*].
youthe n., youth, 3 [O.E. *geoguþ*].
yow pron., you, 35 [O.E. *ēow*].
y-quit v., acquitted, 1 [O.E. *qvit*].

The Franklin's Prologue

aventure n., adventure, occurrence, 38 [O.F. *aventure*].

bare adj., unadorned, 48 [O.E. *bær*].
ben v., are, 54 [O.E. *bēon*].
biginning n., beginning, 45 [O.E. *beginnunge*].

biseche v., beg, 45 [O.E. *bisēcan*].
Briton n., Breton, 37 [O.F. *Breton*].
burel adj., unlettered, plain, 44 [O.F. *burel*].
but prep., except, 52 [O.E. *būtan*].
by-cause conj., because, 44 [O.E. *bi* + O.F. *cause*].

can v., am able, can, 43 [O.E. *cann*].
certeyn adv., indeed, assuredly, 47 [O.F. *certein*].
Cithero n., Cicero, a famous Latin prose-writer, 50 [Lat. *Cicero*].
colour n., colours, ornaments of style, 51 [O.F. *color*].

daye n., day, time, 37 [O.E. *dæg*].
diverse adj., various, different, 38 [O.F. *divers*].
drede n., doubt, fear, 51 [O.E. *drede*].
dye v., dye, 53 [O.E. *deagan*].

elles adv., else, otherwise, 41 [O.E. *elles*].
excuse v., excuse, forgive, 46 [Lat. *excūsare*].

felen v., feel, be moved by, 55 [O.E. *fēlan*].
first adj., earliest, 39 [O.E. *fyrest*].
firste adv., first of all, 45 [O.E. *fyresta*].

gentil adj., kindly, worthy, 37 [O.F. *gentil*].
good adj., good, 43 [O.E. *gōd*].
growen v., grow, be found, 52 [O.E. *grōwan*].

have v., have, 46 [O.E. *habban*].
hem pron., them, 41 [O.E. *him*].
here v., hear, 56 [O.E. *hīeran*].
hir adj., their, 39 [O.E. *hiere*].

instrument n., musical instrument, 40 [Lat. *instrumentum*].

knowe v., know, 51 [O.E. *cnāwan*].

lay n., song, short poem, 38 [O.F. *lai*].
lerne v., learn, 47 [O.E. *leornian*].

list v., it pleases, 56 [O.E. *lystan*].

maden v., p.t. **make**.
make v., make, 38 [O.E. *macian*].
matere n., matters, 55 [O.F. *matiere*].
mede n., meadow, 52 [O.E. *mæd*].
men n., men, people, we, 53 [O.E. *men*].
moot v., must, 48 [O.E. *mōt*].
mount n., mount, mountain, 49 [Lat. *montem*].

ne adv., nor, 50 [O.E. *ne*].
never adv., never, 47 [O.E. *næfre*].
noght pron., nothing, 55 [O.E. *nāht*].
none pron., none, 51 [O.E. *nān*].

olde adj., old, of old time, 37 [O.E. *eald*].
oon adj., one, 42 [O.E. *ān*].

peynte v., paint, 53 [O.F. *peindre*].
plesaunce n., enjoyment, 41 [O.F. *plaisance*].
pleyn adj., unadorned, plain, 48 [O.F. *plein*].

queynt difficult to understand, 54 [O.F. *cointe*].

redden v., read, study, 47 [O.E. *rǣdan*].
remembraunce n., memory, recollection, 42 [O.F. *remembrance*].
rethoryk n., rhetoric, 47 [Gk. *rhetorike*].
rude adj., unrefined, rough, 46 [O.F. *rude*].
ryme v., compose in rhyme, 39 [O.E. *rīman*].

seyn v., say, tell, relate, 43 [O.E. *secgan*].
shal v., shall, 43 [O.E. *sceal*].
shul v., shall, 56 [O.E. *scule*].
sing v., sing [O.E. *singan*].
sire n., gentleman, 44 [O.F. *sire*].
sleep v., sleep, 49 [O.E. *slǣpan*].
songe v., p.t., **singen**, sang, 40 [O.E. *singan*].
speche n., speech, way of speaking, 46 [O.E. *spǣc*].

speke v., speak, tell, 48 [O.E. *specan*].
spirit n., spirit, 55 [O.F. *espirit*].
swiche adj., such, 53 [O.E. *swylc*].

tale n., tale, story, 56 [O.E. *talu*].
they pron., they, 40 [O.E. *þā*].
thing n., anything, 48 [O.E. *þing*].
thise adj., the, these, 37 [O.E. *þes*].
to adv., too, 54 [O.E. *tō*].
tonge n., tongue, language, 39 [O.E. *tunge*].

which adj., which, and these, 40 [O.E. *hwilc*].
wil n., will, intention, 43 [O.E. *willa*].
with prep., with, 40 [O.E. *wiþ*].
withouten prep., without, 51 [O.E. *wiþūtan*].

ye pron., you, 56 [O.E. *gē*].
yow pron., you, 45 [O.E. *ēow*].

The Franklin's Tale

a-begged n., a-begging, 852 [O.E. *on-beggaþ*].
above adv., above, in addition, 67 [O.E. *abufen*].
above prep., above, 44 [O.E. *abufen*].
abyde v., wait, remain, 195 [O.E. *abīdan*].
abyde v., withdraw, 794 [O.E. *abīdan*].
accord n., agreement, 13 [O.F. *acord*].
acord v., agree, 70 [O.F. *accorder*].
acordaunt adj., suitable, 562 [O.F. *acordūnt*].
adoun adv., down, 134 [O.E. *of* + *dūne*].
after prep., in accordance with, 57 [O.E. *æfter*].
agan v., depart, go, end, 476 [O.E. *agān*].
agayn, ageyn adv., any more, once more, back,
    111 [O.E. *ongēan*].
agayn prep., against, 20 [O.E. *ongēan*].
agayns prep., against, 617 [O.E. *ongēanes*].
ago v., p.p. **agān**.
al adj., all, the whole, everything, 18 [O.E. *eall*].

al adv., entirely, just quite, 100 [O.E. *eall*].

al conj., although, 399 [O.E. *eall*].

al pron., everything, 21 [O.E. *eall*].

al be that conj., although, 602 [O.E. *eall + be + þæt*].

aleye n., path, walk, 285 [O.F. *alee*].

allas interj., alas! 125 [O.F. *hélas*].

alle adj., all, 265 [O.E. *ealle*].

allone adj., alone, only, 191 [O.E. *eall + āna*].

almost adv., nearly, 443 [O.E. *eal + mæst*].

Alnath n., Alnath, the name of a star, 553 [Arab. *Alnath*].

als(o) adv., also, 681, 870 [O.E. *eall + swā*].

alwey adv., always, for ever, continually, 108 [O.E. *eall + weg*].

amidde prep., amidst, in the middle of, 774 [O.E. *a + mid*].

amis adv., mistakenly, wrongly, amiss, 52 [O.E. *a + mis*].

amonges prep., amongst, 197 [O.E. *onmanges*].

amorous adj., in love, loving, 490 [O.F. *amorous*].

an prep., on, 121 [O.E. *ān*].

and conj., if, even if, and, 743 [O.E. *and*].

angre n., anger, wroth, distress, strife, misunderstanding, 825 [O. Icel. *angr*].

anon, anoon adv., at once, immediately, 37 [O.E. *on-ān*].

anon-right adv., immediately, 580 [O.E. *onān-riht*].

anoye v., harm, injure, be harmful to, 147 [O.F. *ennuyer*].

answer v., answer, reply, 280 [O.E. *andswerian*].

any adj., any, 22 [O.E. *ǣnig*].

apaye v., please, delight, 820 [O.F. *apaier*].

apparence n., (false) appearance, illusion, 412 [O.F. *apparence*].

arace v., pull away, tear away, 665 [O.F. *esracier*].

areste v., arrest, seize, 642 [O.F. *arester*].

argument n., argument, logical reasoning (see note to 549), 158 [O.F. *argument*].

Aries n., the Ram in the zodiac, 554 [Lat. *Aries*].

armes n., arms, battle, 83 [O.F. *armes*].

array n., dress, 199 [O.F. *arei*].

array v., make beautiful, adorn, appoint, 182 [O.F. *arrier*].

arte n., subject, 392 [O.F. *art*].

artow art thou, 362 [O.E. *eart + þu*].

arwe n., arrow, 384 [O.E. *earh*].

arysing n., time of rising of a planet, 559 [O.E. *ārīsinge*].

as conj., as if, 886 [O.E. *ealswā*].

as interj., pray, 161 [O.E. *ealswā*].

as in prep., as the result of, 29 [O.E. *ealswā + in*].

as wis interj., certainly, indeed, 742 [O.E. *ealswā + wiss*].

ask v., plead for, 230 [O.E. *ascian*].

assaye v., attempt, put to the test, 839 [O.F. *assaier*].

assente v., consent, 656 [O.F. *assentir*].

asterte v., get away from, avoid, 294 [O.F. *æt +* O.N. *sterta*].

astonie v., astound, stun, 611 [O.F. *estonir*].

astrologye n., astrology, 538 [O.F. *astrologie*].

aswage v., lessen, diminish, 107 [O.F. *assouagier*].

at-after prep., after, 190 [O.E. *æt + æfter*].

at al adv., entirely, 208 [O.E. *æt + eall*].

atte prep., at the, 10 [O.E. *æt + þe*].

atteyne v., reach to, attain to, 47 [O.F. *ateindre*].

avantage n., advantage, 44 [O.F. *avantage*].

avaunt n., boast, 848 [O.F. *avant*].

aventure n., fortune, luck, chance, 212 [O.F. *aventure*].

avyse v., consider, 592 [O.F. *aviser*].

await v., wait for, 571 [O.F. *agvaitier*].

awey(e) adv., out of the way, gone, 116, 336 [O.E. *a + wei*].

ay adv., always, 384 [O.N. *ei*].

bacheler n., bachelor, 398 [O.F. *bacheler*].

bad v., p.t. **biddan**, 484 [O.E. *bæd*].

bank n., coast, cliff, 121 [O.N. *bakki*].

bar v., p.t. **bere**, 381 [O.E. *bær*].

bare adj., bare (mere), 296 [O.E. *bær*].

barefoot adj., barefoot, 349 [O.E. *bærfōt*].

barge n., ship, vessel, 122 [O.F. *barge*].

bed, bedde n., bed, 355 [O.E. *bedd*].

been v., p.p. be, 36 [O.E. *bēon*].

beest n., beast, 146 [O.F. *beste*].

begger n., beggar, 836 [O.E. *beggere*].

ben v., did, 649 [O.E. *bēon*].

benignitee n., kindness, 311 [O.F. *benignité*].

berd n., beard, 524 [O.E. *beard*].

bere v., carry, bear, give birth to [O.E. *beran*].

best adv., best [O.E. *betst*].

beste adj., best, 3 [O.E. *betst*].

beste n., best, 118 [O.E. *beste*].

bet adj., better, 694 [O.E. *bet*].

bete v., beat, flap, 38 [O.E. *bēatan*].

be-war v., beware, 813 [O.E. *be-wær*].

biddan v., order, request, 790 [O.E. *biddan*].

biforen adv., before, 865 [O.E. *beforan*].

biforn prep., before, in the sight of, 198 [O.E. *beforan*].

bigan v., p.t. **biginne**, 864.

biginne v., begin, 202 [O.E. *biginnan*].

bigon v., p.p. surround, 588 [O.E. *began*].

bigonne v., p.t. **biginne**, 301.

bihaten v., promise, 60 [O.E. *be-hatan*].

biheste n., promise, 435 [O.E. *behæs*].

bihight v., p.t. **bihaten**, 599.

biholde v., look, stare, 135 [O.E. *behealdan*].

bihoveth v., it is necessary, 631 [O.E. *behofian*].

bileve n., belief, 405 [O.E. *belēafe*].

biloved adj., beloved, 218 [O.E. *beleafod*].

birafte v., p.t. **bireve**, 672.

bireve v., deprive, take away [O.E. *berēafian*].

biseche v., beg, beseech, 846 [O.E. *besēcan*].

bisily adv., eagerly, diligently, 323 [O.E. *bisilīche*].

bisinesse n., diligence, anxiety, care, 99 [O.E. *bisignes*].

bisyde adv., close at hand, 174 [O.E. *bisīden*].

bittre adj., bitter, cruel, 128 [O.E. *biter*].

bitwene prep., between, 825 [O.E. *bitwēonan*].

bitwixe prep., between, 28 [O.E. *bitweox*].

bityde v., happen, occur, 273 [O.E. *betīdan*].

biwreye v., reveal, disclose, 226 [O.Fris. *biwrogia*].

blake adj., black, 140 [O.E. *blæc*].

blede v., bleed, 466 [O.E. *blēdan*].

blisful adj., happy, blessed, merry, joyful, 78 [O.E. *blisful*].

blisse n., happiness, 16 [O.E. *bliss*].

blowe v., blow, 160 [O.E. *blāwan*].

body n., body, 638 [O.E. *bodig*].

bond n., covenant, obligation, 806 [O.E. *bonda*].

book n., book, 479 [O.E. *bōc*].

boot n., boat, 266 [O.E. *bāt*].

born v., p.p. **bere**, 187.

borwe n., pledge, surety, 506 [O.E. *borg*].

boun adj., prepared, ready, on her way, 775 [O.N. *buinn*].

brast v., burst, p.t. **breste**, 752.

braun n., flesh, 526 [O.F. *braon*].

breeth n., breath, 754 [O.E. *brǣð*].

breke v., break, 791 [O.E. *brecan*].

brest n., breast, 381 [O.E. *brēost*].

breste v., burst, break, 31 [O.E. *berstan*].

bresting n., breaking, 245 [O.E. *brestung*].

breyde v., pass, go, take leave of, 299 [O.F. *braire*].

brid n., bird, 146 [O.E. *bridd*].

bringen v., bring, deliver, carry, 531 [O.E. *bringen*].

brinke n., cliff edge, shore, 130 [Swed. *brink*].

broght v., p.p. **bringen**, 355.

brother n., brother, 879 [O.E. *brōþor*].

bugle n., young bull, 525 [O.F. *bugle*].

bugle-horn n., drinking horn, 525 [O.F. *bugle* + O.E. *horn*].

burned adj., burnished, 519 [O.E. *burnir*].

but adv., almost, 309 [O.E. *būtan*].

but conj., unless, except, 75, 311, 387 [O.E. *būtan*].

but-if conj., if not, unless, except for, 184 [O.E. *būtan-if*].

by-cause conj., since, because, 233 [O.E. *bi* + O.F. *cause*].

cacche v., catch, conceive [O.F. *cachier*].

calcule v., calculate, 556 [O.F. *calculer*].

cam v., p.t. **come**, 732.

can v., is able to, know, 270 [O.E. *cann*].

can on v., understand, 58 [O.E. *cann*].

care n., anxiety, distress, 109 [O.E. *caru*].

cas n., circumstance, situation, matter, 98 [O.F. *cas*].

caste v., cast, let fall, 130 [Icel. *kasta*].

castel n., castle, 119 [O.F. *castel*].

caughte v., p.t. **cacche**, 12.

cause n., cause, reason, purpose, 159 [O.F. *cause*].

cause v., cause, bring about, 55 [O.F. *cause*].

causeless adv., for no reason, 97 [O.F. *cause* + O.E. *lēas*].

certein adj., sure, definite, 138 [O.F. *certein*].

certes adv., definitely, indeed, 589 [O.F. *certes*].

certeyn adv., indeed, 45 [O.F. *certein*].

certeyn adj., fixed, definite, 840 [O.F. *certein*].

centre n., point on rete (see note), 549 [O.F. *centre*].

chalange v., claim, 596 [O.F. *chalengier*].

chastitee n., chastity, 716 [O.F. *chastete*].

chaunginge n., change, 54 [O.F. *chaung* + O.E. *inge*].

chees v., p.t. **chese**, 656.

cheke n., cheek, 350 [O.E. *cēace*].

chere n., merriment, entertainment, 370 [O.F. *chere*].

cherisse v., cherish, show respect, 826 [O.F. *cherir*].

cherlish adj., mean, surly, base, 795 [O.E. *ceorlisc*].

ches n., chess, 172 [O.F. *eschecs*].

chese v., choose, 358 [O.E. *cēosan*].

cheyne n., chain, trammles, 628 [O.F. *chaene*].

chiertee n., kindly feeling, kindliness, 153 [O.F. *cherite*].

chirche n., church, 405 [O.E. *cirice*].

chivalrye n., valour, 360 [O.F. *chevalerie*].

chyde v., scold, 48 [O.E. *cīdan*].

citee n., city, 443 [O.F. *cité*].

clene adj., free, 267 [O.E. *clēne*].

clepe v., name, call, 80 [O.E. *cleopian*].

clerk n., scholar, learned person, student, 46 [O.F. *clerc*].

cofre n., coffer, money chest, 843 [O.F. *cofre*].

colde adj., baneful, cold, sorrowful, 136 [O.E. *cald*].

colde v., grow cold, 295 [O.E. *cealdian*].

collect n., table of motion (see note to line 547) [Lat. *collecta*].

come v., come, appear, descend, 7 [O.E. *cuman*].

companye n., company, 654 [O.F. *compaignie*].

compassioun n., compassion, pity, 351 [O.F. *compassioun*].

compleint n., lament, lamentation, 192 [O.F. *complainte*].

complexioun n., temperament, disposition, 54 [O.F. *complexioun*].

complayne v., lament, 263 [O.F. *complaindre*].

compleyning n., (complaining) lament,
217 [O.F. *complein* + O.E. *inge*].

conclude v., conclude, come to a conclusion, form an opinion, 424 [O.F. *concluden*].

conclusioun n., summing up, decision, 161 [O.F. *conclusioun*].

confort n., encouragement, comfort, consolation, 376 [O.F. *confort*].

conforten v., encourage, 95 [O.F. *conforten*].

confusioun n., disorder, confusion, 141 [O.F. *confusion*].

consider v., consider, 555 [O.F. *considerer*].

consolacioun n., comforting, 106 [O.F. *consolatioun*].

constellacioun n., evil influence of the stars, 53 [O.F. *constellacion*].

constreyne v., keep under restraint, 36 [O.F. *constraindre*].

contenance n., appearance, 757 [O.F. *contenance*].

contree n., part of the country, estate, 72 [O.F. *contree*].

convenient adj., suitable, 550 [Lat. *convenientes*].

coost n., coast, 267 [O.F. *coste*].

coppe n., cup, 214 [O.E. *cuppa*].

correct v., adjust, correct, 546 [Lat. *correctum*].

cost v., expenditure, 829 [O.F. *coust*].

coude v., p.t. **can**, 75.

cours n., course of a ship, journey, 123 [O.F. *cours*].

covenant n., agreement, promise, 859 [O.F. *covenant*].

craft n., skill, subject, art, 181 [O.E. *cræft*].

creacioun n., creation, 142 [O.F. *creation*].

creature n., person, 211 [O.F. *creatour*].

crepe v., creep [O.E. *crēopan*].

cropen v., p.p. **crepe**, 886.

crye v., cry, weep, 768 [O.F. *crien*].

cure n., cure, 386 [Lat. *cura*].

curious adj., recondite, magical, occult, 392 [O.F. *curious*].

curiously adv., ingeniously, 181 [O.F. *curious*+O.E. *līce*].

cursednesse n., wickedness, 544 [O.E. *cursednesse*].

curse v., curse, 830 [O.E. *cursian*].

curteisye n., courtesy, consideration, 841 [O.F. *courteisie*].

dar v., dare, 33 [O.E. *dear*].

daunce n., dance, 227 [O.F. *dance*].

daunce v., dance, 172 [O.F. *dancer*].

dawes n., days, 452 [O.E. *dawes*].

day n., day, day of respite, time, life, 18 [O.E. *dæg*].

declinacioun n., declination, distance from celestial equator, 305 [Lat. *declinationem*].

dede adj., dead, 453 [O.E. *dēad*].

dedly adj., mortal, stricken, 312 [O.E. *dēadlīc*].

deed adj., dead, 608 [O.E. *dēad*].

deeth n., death, 294 [O.E. *dēað*].

defaute n., fault, failing, neglect, 62 [O.F. *defaute*].

defoulen v., defile, 668 [O.F. *defoulen*].

degree n., rank, position, 24 [O.F. *degre*].

deitee n., deity, sway, lordship, 319 [O.F. *deite*].

delay n., delay, 566 [O.F. *delai*].

delit n., (lust) pleasure, 644 [O.F. *delit*].

delitable adj., enjoyable, delightful, 171 [O.F. *delitable*].

demen v., impute, judge, give opinion, 758 [O.E. *dēman*].

departe v., separate, divide, break up, 804 [O.F. *despartir*].

dere adj., dear, 686 [O.E. *dēore*].

derke adj., gloomy, 116 [O.E. *deorc*].

descend v., get down, alight, 514 [O.F. *descendre*].

desire v., desire, wish for, 40 [O.F. *desirer*].

desk n., table, 400 [Dut. *disch*].

despeyre v., sink in despair, 215 [O.F. *desperer*].

despyt n., scorn, contempt, 643 [O.F. *despit*].

destroy v., destroy, 148 [O.F. *destruire*].

desyr n., desire, ardour, 321 [O.F. *desier*]

deth n., death, 282 [O.E. *dēað*].

dette n., debt, 850 [O.F. *dette*].

devyse v., relate, tell clearly, detail, 315 [O.F. *deviser*].

deye v., die, 250 [O.N. *deyja*].

deyntee n., dignity, pleasure, 275 [O.F. *deinte*].

dide v., see **doon**, 471 [O.E. *dōn*].

diligence n., level best, utmost, 530 [O.F. *diligence*].

diner n., dinner, 190 [O.F. *disner*].

disconfort v., distress, 168 [O.F. *desconforter*].

discryve v., describe, 203 [O.F. *descrivre*].

disese n., distress, 586 [O.F. *desaise*].

dishonour n., dishonour, shame, disgrace, 630 [O.F. *deshonor*].

dispeyre v., overcome with despair, 356 [O.F. *desperer*].

displese v., displease, 585 [O.F. *desplaisir*].

disport n., diversion, relaxation, pleasure, 167 [O.F. *despartir*].

disporte v., amuse, relax, 121 [O.F. *desporter*].

disputisoun n., argument, disputation, 162 [O.F. *desputoisoun*].

distresse n., suffering, anxiety, grief, 9 [O.F. *destrece*].

diverse adj., different, various, 412 [O.F. *divers*].

do v., make, cause to be done, manage, 250 [O.E. *dōn*].

do v., pp. **do**, 605 [O.E. *dōn*].

doghter n., daughter, 701 [O.E. *dohtor*].

doom n., judgement, 200 [O.E. *dōm*].

doon v., do, provide for, commit, cause, 99 [O.E. *dōn*].

dooth v., does, 52 [O.E. *dēþ*].

dorste v., durst, dared, 8 [O.E. *dorste*].

double adj., forked, 524 [O.F. *duble*].

doun adv., down, 455 [O.E. *dūne*].

dounward adv., downward, 130 [O.E. *dūneweard*].

doute n., fear, 368 [O.F. *doute*].

drawe v., approach, draw near, 237 [O.E. *dragan*].

drede n., fear, doubt, 8 [O.E. *drēde*].

drede v., fear, 584 [O.E. *drēden*].

dredful adj., timorous, full of fear, 581 [O.E. *drēdful*].

drenchen v., drown [O.E. *drencan*].

dreynte v., p.t. **drenchen**, 650.

drive v., drive, complete, 502 [O.E. *drīfan*].

drope n., drop, 612 [O.E. *dropa*].

drough v., p.t. **drawe**, 237 [O.E. *drōh*].

dryve v., drive away, 116 [O.E. *drīfan*].

duren v., remain, continue, 108 [O.F. *durer*].

dwelle v., dwell, stay, 81 [O.E. *dwellan*].

dyen v., die, 587 [O.N. *deyja*].

ech pron., each, 306 [O.E. *ǣlc*].

eek adv., also, 7 [O.E. *ēac*].

eest adv., east, 145 [O.E. *ēast*].

eft adv., again, any more, 825 [O.E. *eft*].

eighte adj., eighth, 552 [O.E. *eahta*].

eke adv., also, 652 [O.E. *ēac*].

ekko n., echo, 223 [Gk. *echo*].

elles adv., else, otherwise, 49 [O.E. *elles*].

emperesse n., empress, ruler, 320 [O.F. *emperice*].

emprente v., imprint, impress, 103 [O.F. *empreinter*].

emprenting n., impression, impress, imprint, 106 [O.F. *empreint* + O.E. *ing*].

empryse n., undertaking, enterprise, 4 [O.F. *emprise*].

ende n., end, 896 [O.E. *ende*].

endelong prep., throughout, 264 [O.E. *and* + *lang*].

endure v., last, continue, bear, 334 [O.F. *endure*].

endyte v., write, relate, tell, 822 [O.F. *enditer*].

enquere v., search for, 651 [O.F. *enqverre*].

ensample n., example, instance, 691 [O.F. *ensample*].

entende v., concern oneself, 369 [O.F. *entendre*].

entente n., meaning, intention, purpose, 231 [O.F. *entente*].

equacion n., equation (see note to 551) [Lat. *æquationem*].

er conj., before, 5 [O.E. *ǣr*].

erst adv., before, 253 [O.E. *ǣrest*].

earthe n., earth, ground, 375 [O.E. *eorðe*].

ese n., content, happiness, comfort, 60 [O.F. *aise*].

eterne adj., eternal, 137 [O.F. *eterne*].

evene adv., regularly, 341 [O.F. *efen*].

ever adv., always, at any time, 734 [O.F. *ǣfre*].

everich pron., each, 34 [O.E. *ǣghwilc*].

everichoon pron., everyone, 101 [O.E. *ǣfre* + *ylc* + *an*].

every adj., each, every, 793 [O.E. *ǣver* + *ǣlc*].

every-deel n., every detail, 560 [O.E. *ǣfre* + *dæl*].

expans adj., separate (see note 547) [Lat. *expansus*].

eyen n., eyes, 130 [O.E. *ēagan*].

face n., sign, 560 [O.E. *face*].

fader n., father, 645 [O.E. *fæder*].

fadme n., fathom, 332 [O.E. *faðme*].

faille v., break promise, fail, 849 [O.F. *faillir*].

fair adj., fair, lovely, 142 [O.E. *fæger*].

faireste adj., most beautiful, 6 [O.E. *fægreste*].

fallen v., fall, come by chance, happen, 634 [O.E. *feallan*].

fals adj., traitorous, untrue, 13 [O.F. *fals*].
fantasye n., imagination, fancy, 116 [O.F. *fantasie*].
fare v., fare, go, prosper, 851 [O.E. *faran*].
farewel interj., farewell, 38 [O.E. *far + well*].
faringe adj., looking, in appearance, 204 [O.E. *far + ing*].
faste adv., very close, 119 [O.E. *faste*].
faste v., abstain from food, 91 [O.E. *fæstan*].
fauconer n., falconer, 468 [O.F. *fauconer*].
fay n., faith, 746 [O.F. *fei*].
feendly adj., hostile, devilish, 140 [O.E. *feound + līce*].
feith n., word, promise, belief, faith, 506 [O.F. *fei*].
felawe n., (friend) fellow student, 397 [O.N. *felagi*].
fer adv., far, 73 [O.E. *feorr*].
fere n., fear, dread, 132 [O.E. *fǣr*].
ferther adv., farther, 449 [O.E. *ferrer*].
feste n., feast, 641 [O.F. *feste*].
fewe adj., few, 798 [O.E. *fēawe*].
figure n., definite shape, 103 [Lat. *figuram*].
fil, **fille** v., p.t. **fallen**, 13.
fixe adj., stationary, unmoved, 554 [Lat. *fixare*].
flood n., flood-tide, 331 [O.E. *flod*].
flour n., flower, 180 [O.F. *fleur*].
flye n., fly, 404 [O.E. *fleoge*].
folie n., foolish notion, 274 [O.F. *folie*].
folk n., people, 683 [O.E. *folc*].
folwe v., follow, agree to, submit to, 21 [O.E. *folgian*].
foot n., step, foot, 375 [O.E. *fot*].
for conj., for [O.E. *for*].
for prep., for, on account of, 48 [O.E. *for*].
forbede v., forbid, 753 [O.E. *forbēodan*].
fordo v., ruin, utterly destroy, 834 [O.E. *fordōn*].
forestes n., forests, 462 [O.F. *forest*].
forlorn adj., lost completely, 829 [O.E. *forloren*].
forme n., condition, state, 433 [O.F. *forme*].
forth adv., henceforth, straightway, onwards, out, 236 [O.E. *forð*].
forthright adv., direct, 775 [O.E. *forð + rihte*].

forthward adv., forwards, straight ahead,
  441 [O.E. *forð + weard*].
Fortune n., Fortune, Fate, 627 [O.F. *Fortune*].
fote n., foot, step, 449 [O.E. *fōt*].
foul adj., evil, 141 [O.E. *fūl*].
franchise n., generosity, 796 [O.F. *franchise*].
free adj., generous, 894 [O.E. *frēo*].
freend n., friend, 34 [O.E. *frēond*].
freendly adj., friendly, kindly, 739 [O.E. *frēond + līc*].
frely adv., readily, 876 [O.E. *frēo + līce*].
fresshe adj., bright, bold, sprightly, 185 [O.E. *fersc*].
fro prep., from, 73 [O.E. *frō*].
frost n., frost, 522 [O.E. *frost*].
frosty adj., frosty, 516 [O.H.G. *frosti*].
ful adv., very, quite, 25 [O.E. *full*].
fulfille v., satisfy, fulfil, 644 [O.E. *fulfyllan*].
fulle n., full, fullest, 341 [O.E. *full*].
furie n., fury, monster, 222 [O.F. *furie*].
furious adj., raging, cruel, 373 [Lat. *furiōsus*].
fy interj., for shame, 499 [O.F. *fī*].
fynal adj., final, 259 [O.F. *final*].
fyr n., fire, 524 [O.E. *fӯr*].
fyve adj., five, 845 [O.E. *fīf*].

gan v., p.t. **ginne**, 251.
gardin n., garden, 174 [O.F. *gardin*].
gardinward n., direction of the garden, 777 [O.F. *gardin +*
  O.E. *weard*].
general adj., general, universal, 217 [O.F. *general*].
gentil adj., chivalrous, kindly, noble, 815 [O.F. *gentil*].
gentillesse n., courtesy, kindness of heart, nobility of soul,
  26 [O.F. *gentilesse*].
gentilly adv., honourably, generously, 880 [O.F. *gentil +*
  O.E. *līce*].
gere n., equipment, contrivance, 548 [O.E. *gearwe*].
gesse v., suppose, imagine, 758 [Ety. dub.]
gete v., get, receive, 838 [O.E. *gietan*].

gilt n., fault, responsibility, guilt, 29 [O.E. *gylt*].

giltless adj., innocent, guiltless, 590 [O.E. *gylt + lēas*].

ginne v., begin, 251 [O.E. *ginnan*].

glad adj., cheerful, 739 [O.E. *glæd*].

glade v., gladden, make happy, 240 [O.E. *gladian*].

gladly adv., willingly, enthusiastically, 497 [O.E. *glad + līce*].

glyde v., pass, flow, 687 [O.E. *glīdan*].

go(n) v., go, walk, 489 [O.E. *gān*].

God n., God almighty, 28 [O.E. *God*].

goddesse n., goddess, 325 [O.E. *god* + O.F. *esse*].

gon v., p.p. **goon**, 38 [O.E. *gān*].

goon v., go, prosper, go on your way, 81 [O.E. *gān*].

gonne v., p.t. **ginne**, 190.

goth v., pres. **goon**, 618.

goth v., impera. **goon**, 760.

governaunce n., self-control, restraint, rule,
  58 [O.F. *gouvernaunce*].

governour n., ruler, controller, 303 [O.F. *gouverneur*].

grace n., favour, boon, mercy, good fortune, 230 [O.F. *grace*].

graunte v., consent to, permit, grant, 262 [O.F. *granter*].

graven v., engrave, 102 [O.E. *grafan*].

greet adj., great, 25 [O.E. *great*].

grene n., grass, 134 [M.H.G. *gruene*].

gret(e) see **greet**, 188.

grette v., greet, 446 [O.E. *grātan*].

grevaunce n., grief, distress, 213 [O.F. *grevance*].

greve v., harm, distress, 406 [O.F. *grever*].

grim adj., fierce, 418 [O.E. *grimm*].

grisly adj., grim, terrible, cruel, 131 [O.E. grīslie).

grounde n., ground, 541 [O.E. *grund*].

guerdon n., reward, 245 [O.F. *guerdon*].

had v., p.t. sing. **have**.

hadden v., p.t. pl. **have**.

half adv., half, more or less, 783 [O.E. *healf*].

halke n., corner, nook, hiding place, 393 [O.E. *healoe*].

halle n., hall, 415 [O.E. *heall*].

han v., pres. t., have.

hand n., hand, 600 [O.E. *hand*].

happe v., happen, chance, 614 [Icel. *happ*].

harm n., harm, injury, evil, 758 [O.E. *hearm*].

hastily adv., without delay, 111 [O.F. *hastif* + O.E. *līce*].

hastow v., hast thou, 861 [O.E. *hafast* + *ðu*].

haten v., be called, named, 660 [O.E. *hatte*].

hath v., pres. **have**, 677.

hauke n., hawk, 469 [O.E. *hafoc*].

have v., have, accept, 10 [O.E. *habban*].

heed n., head, 554 [O.E. *hēafod*].

heep n., number, 765 [O.E. *hēap*].

heer adv., here, 31 [O.E. *hēr*].

heer-biforn adv., formerly, 807 [O.E. *hēr* + *biforan*].

heer-of adv., hereof, 691 [O.E. *hēr* + *of*].

heet v., p.p. **haten**, 660.

heigh adj., noble, distinguished, exalted, 7 [O.E. *heah*].

helde v., p.t. **holde**.

hele n., prosperity, 359 [O.E. *hælu*].

helle n., hell, 165 [O.E. *hell*].

helpen v., help, 314 [O.E. *helpan*].

hem pron., them, 177 [O.E. *him*].

hemself pron., himself, themselves, 682 [O.E. *him* + *self*].

hemselven pron., themselves, 650 [O.E. *hemselven*].

henten v., seize, 663 [O.E. *hentan*].

herberwe n., 'house' in the heavens, 307 [O.H.G. *heriberga*].

here pron., her, 62 [O.E. *hiere*].

here v., hear, 225 [O.E. *hīeran*].

heritage n., inheritance, 835 [O.F. *heritage*].

herkne v., listen to, 768 [M.E. *hērcnian*].

herne n., corner, nook, 393 [O.E. *hyrne*].

heron n., heron, 469 [O.E. *hairon*].

herte n., heart, 31 [O.E. *heorte*].

herte n., hart, 463 [O.E. *heort*].

heste n., promise, 336 [O.E. *hæs*].

hethen n., heathen, 565 [O.E. *hǣðen*].

hevene n., heaven, 296 [O.E. *heofon*].

hevinesse n., grief, sorrow, distress, 100 [O.E. *hefig* + *nesse*].

hevy adj., heavy, sorrowful, 94 [O.E. *hefig*].

hewe n., hue, colour, tint, 288 [O.E. *hīw*].

hewe v., colour, 517 [O.E. *hīwian*].

hight(e) v., p.t. **hote**, 595.

hir adj., pron., her, their, herself, 14 [O.E. *hiera*].

hire pron., her, 62, 368 [O.E. *hiere*].

hirself, hirselven pron., herself, 624 [O.E. *hire + self*].

his pron., his, its, 128 [O.E. *his*].

holde v., hold, keep, consider, take, carry out, 188 [O.E. *healdan*].

holpe v., p.t. **helpen**.

holpen v., p.p. **helpan**.

hom see **hoom**.

hond n., hand, 805 [O.E. *hand*].

hondred adj., hundred, 465 [O.E. *hundred*].

honour n., honour, reputation, 83 [O.F. *honor*].

honour v., honour, 724 [O.F. *honōrer*].

hool adj., whole, unscathed, 383 [O.E. *hāl*].

hool adv., wholly, entirely, 722 [O.E. *hāl*].

hoom n., home, 72 [O.E. *hām*].

hope n., hope, 196 [O.E. *hopa*].

horrible adj., horrible, 282 [O.F. *horrible*].

hote adj., hot, 518 [O.E. *hāt*].

hote v., promise, be called, 595 [O.E. *hāten*].

hound n., dog, 465 [O.E. *hund*].

housbonde n., husband, 14 [O.E. *hūsbonda*].

how-ever conj., however, 851 [O.E. *hu + æfre*].

humble adj., humble, modest, 63 [O.F. *humble*].

humblesse n., humility, meekness, 25 [O.F. *humblesse*].

hundred n., hundred, 845 [O.E. *hundred*].

hye adj., tall, high, 463 [O.E. *hēah*].

hyeste adj., highest, most solemn, 333 [O.E. *hīehsta*].

illusion n., illusion, false show, 536 [O.F. *illusion*].

image n., image, statue, 663 [O.E. *imāge*].

imaginatif adj., suspicious, 366 [O.F. *imaginatif*].

innocence n., lack of realization of wrong-doing,
873 [O.F. *innocence*].

inpossible n., impossibility, 281 [O.F. *impossible*], adj.,
impossible, 821 [O.F. *impossible*].

ire n., anger, 53 [O.F. *ire*].

jalousie n., jealousy, 20 [O.F. *gelosie*].

japes n., tricks, jests, 543 [Ety. dub.].

jogelrye n., jugglery, conjuring trick, 537 [O.F. *joglerie*].

jolyer adj., gayer, 199 [O.F. *joliere*].

joye n., joy, 291 [O.F. *joie*].

jupartie n., peril, hazard, 767 [O.F. *jeu + parti*].

juste v., joust, tilt, 370 [O.F. *jouster*].

kene adj., keen, sharp, 384 [O.E. *cēne*].

kepe v., preserve, keep safe, 161 [O.E. *cēpan*].

kinde n., nature, kind, 40 [O.E. *cynd*].

kinrede n., kindred, family, lineage, 7 [O.E. *cyn + raeden*].

kirtel v., tunic, kirtle, 852 [O.E. *cyrtel*].

knee n., knee, 114 [O.E. *cnēo*].

knight n., knight, 17 [O.E. *cniht*].

knowe n., knee, 297 [O.E. *cnēo*].

knowe v., know, 452 [O.E. *cnāwan*].

knit v., united, knit, in agreement, 258 [O.E. *cnyttan*].

kythe v., show, display, 20 [O.E. *cȳðhn*].

labour n., task, occupation, 4 [O.F. *labour*].

lady n., lady, wife, 68 [O.E. *hlāfdige*].

lakken v., lack, be wanting, 458 [M. Du. *laken*].

lamentacioun n., lamentation, grief, 788 [O.F. *lamentation*].

langour n., sickness, disease, 373 [O.F. *langour*].

languissh v., grow feeble, suffer pain, 222 [O.F. *langvir*].

large adj., wide, large, 27 [O.F. *large*].

lasse adj., less, 496 [O.E. *lǣssa*].

laste adj., last, 10 [O.E. *laste*].

lasten v., last, endure, 754 [O.E. *lǣstan*].

lat v., allow, let, permit, 274 [O.E. *lǣtan*].

latoun n., brass, bronze, 517 [O.F. *laton*].

lay n., song, love poem, 219 [O.F. *lai*].

lecherye n., lust, [O.F. *lecherie*].

lede v., lead, spend, guide, govern, 16 [O.E. *lǣdan*].

leeste adj., least, 689 [O.E. *lǣst*].

leet v., allow, let, 687 [O.E. *lǣtan*].

lenger adj., adv., longer, 437 [O.E. *lengra*].

leoun n., lion; constellation of Leo, 330, 418 [O.F. *leoun*].

lerne v., learn, 50 [O.E. *leornian*].

lese v., lose, forfeit, 632 [O.E. *losian*].

lesse adj., less, smaller, 326 [O.E. *lǣssa*].

leste adj., least, 436 [O.E. *lǣst*].

leste v., it pleases, 157 [O.E. *lystan*].

lete v., allow, permit, let, leave, cause, 196 [O.E. *lǣtan*].

lette v., prevent, hinder, 266 [O.E. *lettan*].

lettre n., letter, 110 [Lat. *litteram*].

leve adj., dear, 879 [O.E. *lēof*].

leve n., leave, departure, 611 [O.E. *leaf*].

leve n., leaf of a tree, 180 [O.E. *lēaf*].

leve v., give up, abandon, 100 [O.E. *lǣfan*].

lever adj., more pleasing, 795 [O.E. *leovere*].

lever adv., more willingly, rather, 632 [O.E. *lēofra*].

lewed adj., foolish, stupid, wanton, heartless, unfeeling, 766 [O.E. *lǣwede*].

leyser n., leisure, opportunity, 249 [O.F. *leisir*].

libertee n., liberty, freedom, 40 [O.F. *liberte*].

lighte adj., light, happy, joyful, 186 [O.E. *lēoht*].

lighte v., alight, dismount, 455 [O.E. *līhtan*].

lighten v., light up, make cheerful, rejoice, make shine, 322 [O.E. *lēohtan*].

likerous adj., eager, desirous, 391 [O.F. *liquoreux*].

lisse n., relief, comfort, 510 [O.E. *liss*].

lisse v., relieve, comfort, 442 [O.E. *lissian*].

liste v., it pleases, 123 [O.E. *lystan*].

liven v., live, 680 [O.E. *lifian*].

lo interj., lo, indeed, consider, look, 639 [O.E. *lā*].

loke v., look, consider, notice, heed, 43 [O.E. *lōcian*].

longe adj., long, 177 [O.E. *long*].

longen v., belong, 403 [O.E. *langian*].

looth adj., displeasing, hateful, 791 [O.E. *lāð*].

lord n., lord, 14 [O.E. *hlāford*].

lordinges n., my lords, gentlemen, sirs, 893 [O.E. *hlāfording*].

lordshipe n., authority, lordship, 15 [O.E. *hlāfordscipe*].
lorn adj., lost, forlorn, 309 [O.E. *loren*].
lothest adj., most unwilling, most loth, 585 [O.E. *lāðest*].
love n., lover, beloved, 194 [O.E. *lēof*].
love v., love, 276 [O.E. *lufian*].
lovere n., lover, 22 [O.E. *lufu* + *er*].
lowe adv., low, 307 [O.N. *lāgr*].
lust n., desire, pleasure, delight, 84 [O.E. *lust*].
lusty adj., worthy, valiant, 209 [O.E. *lustig*].
lye v., speak untruly, lie, 842 [O.E. *lēogan*].
lye v., remain, stay, rest, lie, 357 [O.E. *licgan*].
lyf n., life, 18 [O.E. *līf*].
lyk adj., like, similar to, 152 [O.E. *gelīc*].
lyke v., impers. it pleases, 90 [O.E. *līcian*].
lym n., lime, 421 [O.E. *lim*].
lyth v., pres. **lye**, 609 [O.E. *licgan*].
lyve n., life, 204 [O.E. *līf*].
lyves n., lives, 16 [O.E. *lif*].

maad v., p.t. **make**, 186.
mad adj., mad, 780 [O.E. *mād*].
madame n., lady, madame, 239 [O.F. *madame*].
magicien n., wonder-worker, 456 [O.F. *magicien*].
magik n., magic, 427 [O.F. *magique*].
maister n., master, expert, 474 [O.F. *maistre*].
maistrye n., authority, mastery, domination, 19 [O.F. *maistrie*].
make v., make, cause, 428 [O.E. *macian*].
man n., one, any one, a man, 15 [O.E. *man*].
maner n., kind of, 702 [O.F. *maniere*].
manere n., manner, way, kind of, 225 [O.F. *maniere*].
mankinde n., mankind, human race, 148 [O.E. *mancynn*].
mansioun n., sphere of influence, 402 [O.F. *mansion*].
manye adj., many, 126 [O.E. *manig*].
matere n., material, subject, topic, 219 [O.F. *matiere*].
may v., may, am able to, can, 108 [O.E. *mæg*].
May n., the month of May, 178 [O.F. *mai*].
mayde n., maiden, maid, maidservant, 637 [O.E. *mægde*].
mayden n., maiden, 647 [O.E. *mægden*].

maydenhede n., virginity, 648 [O.E. *mægdenhad*].
mede n., meadow, field, 419 [O.E. *mæd*].
meke adj., humble, 11 [O.N. *miukr*].
men pron., we, some one, 48 [O.E. *men*].
mene method, means, instrument, 155 [O.F. *moyen*].
menen v., mean, intend, purpose, 253 [O.E. *mēnan*].
merciable adj., merciful, kindly, piteous, 308 [O.F. *merciablé*].
mercy n., mercy, 747 [O.F. *merci*].
merk n., likeness, image, 152 [O.E. *meare*].
merveille n., marvel, wonder, 616 [O.F. *merveille*].
merveillous adj., marvellous, wonderful, 478 [O.F. *merveillos*].
meschaunce n., ill-luck, misfortune, 564 [O.F. *meschance*].
mete v., meet [O.E. *metan*].
mette v., p.t. **mete**, 445.
mighte v., might, could, 240 [O.E. *mihte*].
might n., power, might, 882 [O.E. *miht*].
minde n., mind, 426 [O.E. *mynd*].
miracle n., miracle, 328 [O.F. *miracle*].
mirour n., pattern, example, 726 [O.F. *mireour*].
mo adv., more, 684 [O.E. *mā*].
mone n., moan, lament, 192 [O.E. *man*].
mone n., moon, 426 [O.E. *mōna*].
monstre n., monstrosity, marvel (disaster), 616 [O.F. *monstre*].
moorne v., mourn, lament, 91 [O.E. *murnan*].
moot v., must, 34 [O.E. *mot*].
more adj., more, greater, 326 [O.E. *māra*].
more adv., more, 16 [O.E. *māra*].
morwe n., morning, 178 [O.E. *morgen*].
morwe-tyde n., morning time, 173 [O.E. *morgen* + *tīde*].
moste adv., most, 894 [O.E. *mǣst*].
moste v., must, 195 [O.E. *moste*].
muche adv., much, 290 [O.E. *mycel*].
muchel adv., much, 401 [O.E. *mycel*].
myn adj., my, 31 [O.E. *mīn*].
my-selven pron., myself, 634 [O.E. *me* + *self*].

name n., name, word, reputation, good name, 23 [O.E. *nama*].
namely adv., especially, 11 [O.E. *nama* + *līce*].

na-more adv., no more, any more, 738 [O.E. *nā + māre*].

nas v., was not, 612 [O.E. *ne + was*].

nat adv., not, 36 [O.E. *nāt*].

nathelees adv., nevertheless, notwithstanding, 195 [O.E. *nā + ðȳ + læs*].

naturel adj., natural, 427 [O.F. *naturel*].

naturelly adv., by its very nature, 324 [O.F. *naturel + līce*].

nay interj., no, 742 [O.N. *nai*].

ne adv., not, 145 [O.E *ne*].

neclicence n., negligence, carelessness, 504 [O.F. *negligence*].

nedes adv., necessarily, 435 [O.E. *nēdes*].

nedeth v., is necessary, 738 [O.E. *nēdan*].

neighebour n., neighbour, 233 [O.E. *neāhgebūr*].

nere v., were not, 586 [O.E. *ne + were*].

never adv., never, 18 [O.E. *næfre*].

never-mo adv., never, 348 [O.E. *næfre + mā*].

next adv., on the next occasion, 329 [O.E. *nest*].

newe adj., new, 287 [O.E. *nēowe*].

night n., night, 508 [O.E. *niht*].

nis v., is not, 146 [O.E. *ne + is*].

niste v., knew not, 300 [O.E. *ne + wiste*].

no adj., no, not any, 764 [O.E. *nō*].

noble adj., splendid, worthy, 90 [O.F. *noble*].

noght adv., not at all, 369 [O.E. *nāht*].

noght pron., nothing, 546 [O.E. *nāht*].

nolde v., would not, 764 [O.E. *ne + wolde*].

noon adv., not at all, 50 [O.E. *nān*].

noon pron., no one, 654 [O.E. *nān*].

noon adj., no, 406 [O.E. *nān*].

nothing adv., not at all, in no way, 218 [O.E. *nō + ðing*].

nothing n., nothing, 139 [O.E. *nō + ðing*].

Nowel n., Christmas, 527 [O.F. *Noel*].

ny adv., nearly, nigh, 508 [O.E. *neāh*].

o adj., one, 33 [O.E. *ān*].

obeye v., obey, 21 [O.F. *obier*].

obeysaunce n., deference, submission, 11 [O.F. *obeisaunce*].

observaunce n., customary attentions, 228 [O.F. *observaunce*].

obstacle n., hindrance, 572 [O.F. *obstacle*].
odour n., scent, 185 [O.F. *odor*].
of prep., of, from, by, in respect of, 15 [O.E. *of*].
ofte adv., often, 125.
oght n., pron., anything, 741 [O.E. *ōht*].
oghte v., *ought*, 669 [O.E. *āhte*].
old adj., old, former, 425 [O.E. *eald*].
on prep., on, 472 [O.E. *on*].
only adv., only, 630 [O.E. *ān + līce*].
on-lyve adv., alive, 204 [O.E. *on + līfe*].
oon adj., one, 6 [O.E. *ān*].
operacioun n., movement, working, 401 [O.F. *operation*].
opposicioun n., opposition in the heavens, 329 [O.F. *opposicion*].
oppresse v., violate, rape, 683 [O.F. *oppresser*].
ordinaunce n., provision, preparation, 175 [O.F. *ordenance*].
orisonte n., horizon, 289 [O.F. *orisonte*].
orisoun n., prayer, 298 [O.F. *oreisoun*].
other adj., other, 176 [O.E. *ōðer*].
oute adv., away, abroad, 367 [O.E. *ūt*].
outher conj., either, 29 [O.E. *āwðer*].
over prep., over, 15 [O.E. *ōfer*].
overspringe v., rise above, 332 [O.E. *ōfer + springan*].
owene adj., own, 152 [O.E. *āgen*].

pacience n., patience, endurance, 45 [O.F. *patience*].
pacient adj., patient, long-suffering, 43 [O.F. *patient*].
pale adv., wanly, palely, dimly, 521 [O.F. *pale*].
paradys n., paradise, 184 [O.F. *paradis*].
paraventure adv., perchance, perhaps, 227 [O.F. *par aventure*].
parcel n., part, 124 [O.F. *parcelle*].
pardee interj., by heaven, 717 [O.F. *par dieu*].
parfit adj., perfect, 143 [O.F. *parfit*].
park n., park, 462 [O.F. *parc*].
particuler adj., unusual, recondite, 394 [O.F. *particulier*].
passinge adj., surpassing, excelling, 201 [O.F. *passing*].
pavement n., pavement, floor, 646 [O.F. *pavement*].
paye v., pay, 840 [O.E. *paier*].
payne n., utmost, level best, 2 [O.F. *peine*].

penaunce n., suffering, torment, 12 [O.F. *peneance*].

peny n., penny, 888 [O.E. *penig*].

perilous adj., dangerous, 386 [O.F. *perilleus*].

peyne n., suffering, distress, pain, 9 [O.F. *peine*].

peynt v., paint, 178 [O.F. *peindre*].

Phebus n., the sun, 517 [Lat. *Phebus*].

philosophre n., learned man, philosopher, 833 [O.F. *philosophe*].

pitee n., pity, sympathy, 12 [O.F. *pité*].

pitous adj., sorrowful, full of pity, 166 [O.F. *pitous*].

pitously adv., in sorrow, in pity, sadly, sorrowfully, 135 [O.F. *pitous + līce*].

playn n., plain, level, space, 470 [O.F. *plaigne*].

plesaunce n., delight, amusement, 189 [O.F. *plaisance*].

pley n., play, jest, banter, 260 [O.E. *plega*].

pleyen v., play, amuse oneself, perform, 169 [O.E. *plegian*].

pleyne v., complain against, lament, 48 [O.F. *plaindre*].

pleynt n., petition, 301 [O.E. *plainte*].

plighte v., pledge, 809 [O.E. *plihtan*].

possibilitee n., possibility, 615 [O.F. *possibilité*].

prechen v., give advice, exhort, 96 [O.F. *precher*].

preye v., beg, entreat, pray, 530 [O.F. *preier*].

prively adv., privately, secretly, 13 [O.F. *privē + līce*].

proces n., process of time, 101 [O.F. *proces*].

profre v., offer, set before one, 27 [O.F. *proferer*].

proporcioun n., proportion, calculation, 558 [O.F. *proporcioun*].

proporcionales n., proportional parts, 550 [O.F. *proportciounal*].

prosperitee n., happy state, content, 71 [O.F. *prosperite*].

prys n., excellence, high esteem, 183 [O.F. *pris*].

pured adj., refined, pure, 832 [O.F. *pured*].

purposinge v., intending, purposing, 730 [O.F. *proposer*].

purveyaunce n., providence, providing, things needed, 137 [O.F. *purveaunce*].

quake v., quake, tremble, 132 [O.E. *cwākien*].

quene n., queen, 318 [O.E. *cwēn*].

question n., question, 893 [O.F. *question*].

quiete n., content, peace, 32 [O.F. *qviete*].

quik adj., alive, living, 608 [O.E. *cwic*].

quiken v., endow with life, 322 [O.E. *cwician*].
quikkest adj., busiest, 774 [O.E. *cwicest*].
quit adj., discharged from, 806 [O.E. *quite*].
quit v., release, discharge, set free, 635 [O.F. *qviten*].
quod v., said, quoth, 252 [O.E. *cwaþ*].

rage n., anguish, deep sorrow, grief, 108 [O.F. *rage*].
rather adv., preferably, rather, 669 [O.E. *hraþur*].
raving n., lack of self-control, delirium, 299 [O.F. *raver*].
reaven v., rob, plunder, deprive of, 289 [O.E. *rēafian*].
rede adj., red, 420 [O.E. *rēad*].
reden v., read, study, 392 [O.E. *rǣdan*].
redresse v., avenge a wrong, 708 [O.F. *redresser*].
redy adj., ready, 482 [M.L.G. *rēdig*].
reft v., p.p. **reaven**.
regioun n., region, 346 [O.F. *region*].
reherce v., repeat, go over again, 738 [O.F. *rehercer*].
relesse v., release, give back, 805 [O.F. *relesser*].
remembraunce n., memory, recollection,
  389 [O.F. *remembrance*].
remembre v., remind, recall to memory, 515 [O.F. *remembrer*].
remenant n., remainder, 558 [O.F. *remanant*].
remoeve v., remove, 493 [Lat. *removere*].
repent v., repent, 593 [O.F. *repentir*].
repreve v., find fault with, reprove, 809 [O.F. *reprever*].
requeste n., request, 117 [O.F. *requeste*].
resoun n., reasoning, advice, 105 [O.F. *raisoun*].
respyten v., grant a respite, 854 [O.F. *respiter*].
reste n., peace, repose, 490 [O.E. *rest*].
revel n., revelry, merrymaking, display, 287 [O.F. *revel*].
reverence n., respect, regard, obedience, 529 [O.F. *reverence*].
rewe v., have pity, 246 [O.E. *hrēowan*].
reyn n., rain, 522 [O.E. *regn*].
reyne n., kingdom, reign, 27 [O.F. *regne*].
riche adj., rich, powerful, 205 [O.E. *rice*].
right adv., exceedingly, straight, very, just, quite,
  136 [O.E. *rihte*].
right n., justice, privilege, 596 [O.E. *riht*].

righte adj., true, direct, nearest, 512 [O.E. *riht*].

rigour n., strictness, severity, determination, 47 [O.F. *rigour*].

rivere n., river, hawking ground, 170 [O.F. *riviere*].

rokke n., rock, 131 [O.F. *roche*].

romen v., stroll, wander, roam, 115 [O.H.G. *rämen*].

rote n., root, basic data, 548 [O.N. *rot*].

roundel n., roundel (see note), 220 [O.F. *rondel*].

routhe n., pity, compassion, distress, 533 [M.E. *hrēouthe*].

rowen v., row a boat, 417 [O.E. *rōwan*].

sake n., sake, 164 [O.E. *sacu*].

salewe v., greet, address, 582 [O.F. *saluer*].

sauf adj., safe, 315 [O.F. *sauf*].

saufly adv., safely, without contradiction, 33 [O.F. *sauf* + *līche*].

saugh v., p.t. **see**, 118.

save prep., save, except, 23, 216 [O.F. *sauf*].

save v., save, keep, preserve, 750 [O.F. *sauver*].

say v., p.t. **see**, 396.

sayd v., p.p. **seyen**, 819.

sayn v., say, record, repeat, 691 [O.E. *secgan*].

science n., a branch of knowledge, 394 [O.F. *science*].

secree adv., secretly, 381 [O.F. *secroi*].

see n., sea, 119 [O.E. *sǣ*].

see(n) v., see, 63 [O.E. *seon*].

seeth v., pres. **seen**, 294.

seide v., p.t. **seye(n)**, 867.

seigh v., p.t. **seen**, 122.

seilien v., sail, 123 [O.E. *seglian*].

seith v., pres. **seyen**, 52.

seke v., seek, 83 [O.E. *sēcan*].

selle v., sell, 835 [O.E. *sellan*].

selve adj., same, 666 [O.E. *self*].

semen v., seem, appear, 141 [O.E. *sēman*].

servage n., servitude, 66 [O.F. *servage*].

servant n., servant, lover, devotee, 64 [O.F. *servant*].

serve v., serve, 3 [O.F. *servir*].

service n., devotion, 244 [O.F. *servise*].

sesoun n., season, 306 [O.F. *saison*].

seten v., sit, 480 [O.E. *settan*].

sette v., p.t. **sitte**, 297.

sette v., devote, esteem, place, 84 [O.E. *settan*].

seurtee n., surely, security, 853 [O.F. *surete*].

sevene adj., seven, 681 [O.E. *seofon*].

seyde v., p.t. **seyen**, 848.

seye(n) v., say, tell, declare, 33 [O.E. *secgan*].

seyth v., impera. of **seyen**, 799.

shal v., must, ought to, will, 22 [O.E. *sceal*].

shame n., disgrace, shame, good name, 24 [O.E. *scamu*].

shame v., bring shame upon, 436 [O.E. *scamian*].

shapen v., prepare, arrange, 169 [O.E. *scieppan*].

sheene adj., bright, 317 [O.E. *scene*].

ship n., ship, 122 [O.E. *scip*].

sholde v., should, ought to, would, 19 [O.E. *scolde*].

shoon v., p.t. **shyne**, 519 [O.E. *scīnan*].

shoop v., p.t. **shapen**, 81.

shopen v., p.t. **shapen**, 169.

shortly adv., in a few words, briefly, 207 [O.E. *sceort + līce*].

shoure n., shower, 179 [O.E. *scur*].

shove v., move, push, 553 [O.E. *scufan*].

shul v., shall, must, 50 [O.E. *sceal*].

shyne v., shine [O.E. *scīnan*].

sighte n., appearance, look, 185 [O.H.G. *sīht*].

signe n., sign of the zodiac, 330 [O.F. *signe*].

siker adj., certain, sure, 411 [O.E. *sicor*].

sikerly adv., surely, certainly, 850 [O.E. *sicor + līce*].

siknesse n., sickness, illness, [O.E. *sēoc + nesse*].

sin conj., since, 263 [O.E. *siþþan*].

sinken v., sink, 164, 541 [O.E. *sincan*].

sire n., sir, sire, 26 [O.F. *sire*].

sith conj., since, 26 [O.E. *siþ*].

sitte v., sit, 129 [O.E. *sittan*].

sixte adj., sixth, 178 [O.E. *sixta*].

skippe v., jump, leap, 674 [Ety. Dub.].

slake v., abate, 113 [O.E. *slacian*].

slayn v., p.p. **slee(n)**, 112.

slee(n) v., slay, kill [O.E. *slēan*].

sleet n., sleet, 522 [O.E. *slēt*].

sleeth v., pres. **sleen**, 97.

slepen v., sleep, 744 [O.E. *slēpan*].

slitte v., pierce, cut, split, slit, 532 [O.E. *slīten*].

slouthe n., sloth, slackness, 504 [O.E. *slǣwð*].

slow v., p.t. **sleen**, 687.

slyde v., slip away, depart, 196 [O.E. *slīdan*].

smerte adj., severe, bitter, cruel, 246 [O.E. *smeart*].

smerte n., anguish, 128 [M.L.G. *smerte*].

so adv., in the same way [O.E. *swā*].

so conj., so long as, if, 240 [O.E. *swā*].

sobrely adv., gravely, calmly, 857 [O.F. *sobre* + *līce*].

socour n., help, relief, remedy, 629 [O.F. *socors*].

sodein adj., sudden, 282 [O.F. *soudain*].

sodeinly adv., quickly, 287 [O.F. *soudain* + *līce*].

softe adj., soft, gentle, 179 [O.E. *sēfte*].

solas n., ease, comfort, content, 74 [O.F. *solaz*].

som adj., some, 103 [O.E. *sum*].

somme adj., some, 103 [O.E. *sum*].

somme n., sum of money, 492 [O.F. *somme*].

somme pron., some, 466 [O.E. *sum*].

somtyme adv., some time or other, occasionally, 52 [O.E. *sum* + *tīma*].

somwhat adv., to some extent, somewhat, 216 [O.E. *sum* + *hwæt*].

somwher adv., somewhere, 169 [O.E. *sum* + *hwēre*]

songe n., song, 220 [O.E. *song*].

sonken v., p.p. **sinken**.

sonne n., sun, 6 [O.E. *sunne*].

soor adj., sore, sad, aching, 843 [O.E. *sār*].

sopeer n., supper, 461 [O.F. *soper*].

sore adv., sadly, in sorrow, bitterly, 278 [O.E. *sare*].

sorwe n., sorrow, grief, distress, 107 [O.E. *sorg*].

sorweful adj., sorrowful, 136 [O.E. *sorh* + *ful*].

sorwefully adv., sorrowfully, 862 [O.E. *sorhful* + *līche*].

soth n., truth, 42 [O.E. *sōð*].

sothe n., truth, 207 [O.E. *sōð*].

soule n., soul, 255 [O.E. *sāwol*].

soupe v., take supper, 489 [O.F. *souper*].

soveraynetee n., supremacy, lordship, 23 [O.F. *soverainete*].

sovereyn adj., supreme, highest, 582 [O.F. *soverain*].

spak v., p.t. **speken**, 300.

speche n., conversation, 236 [O.E. *spǣc*].

spedde v., p.t. **speden**, 534.

speden v., hasten, hurry, [O.E. *spēdan*].

speken v., speak, 55 [O.E. *specan*].

spere n., sphere, 552 [M.E. *espere*].

spring adj., spring, 342 [O.E. *springe*].

springe v., spring up, 419 [O.E. *springan*].

spye v., notice, see, spy, 778 [O.F. *espier*].

squyer n., squire (attendant), esquire, manservant, 198, 481 [O.F. *esqvier*].

stable adj., unchanging, steadfast, 143 [O.F. *estable*].

standan v., stand, be placed [O.E. *standan*].

stant v., pres. **standan**, 526.

stike v., stab, pierce, 748 [O.E. *stician*].

stille adj., still, without moving, quiet, [O.E. *stille*].

stinten v., cease, 86 [O.E. *styntan*].

stirten v., start up, spring up, rush, 440 [O.E. *stertan*].

stoon n., stone, 102 [O.E. *stān*].

storie n., story, 684 [O.F. *estoire*].

straunge adj., difficult, 495 [O.F. *estrange*].

streme n., beam of light, ray, 519 [O.E. *strēam*].

strete n., street, 774 [O.E. *strǣt*].

strong adj., strong, 205 [O.E. *strong*].

stryf n., strife, quarrelling, 29 [O.F. *estrife*].

studie n., place of study, 395 [O.F. *estudie*].

subtile adj., ingenious, clever, shrewd, 413 [Lat. *sub + tela*].

subtilly adv., skilfully, 556 [Lat. *sub + tela + līce*].

suffrance n., forbearance, consideration, 60 [O.F. *sufrance*].

suffre v., endure, put up with, 49 [O.F. *sufrir*].

supersticious adj., diabolical, 544 [O.F. *superstitieux*].

surement n., pledge, oath, promise, 807 [O.F. *seurement*].

surgerye n., surgery, 386 [O.F. *cirurgerie*].

sursanure n., wound healed outwardly only, 385 [Ety. dub.].

sustene v., hold up, support, 133 [O.F. *sustenir*].

suster n., sister, 317 [O.E. *sweostor*].

swerd n., sword, 532 [O.E. *sweord*].

swere v., swear, 61 [O.E. *swerian*].

swete adj., dear one, love, 250 [O.E. *swēte*].

swich adj., such, so great, such-and-such, 12 [O.E. *swylc*].

swoor v., p.t. **swere**, 17.

sworn v., p.p. **swere**.

swowne n., swoon, faint, 352 [O.E. *swōgan*].

swyn n., swine, boar, 526 [O.E. *swīn*].

syde n., side, 793 [O.E. *sīde*].

syke adj., sick, 372 [O.E. *sēoc*].

syke n., sigh, 136 [O.E. *sice*].

syke v., sigh, 89 [O.E. *sīcan*].

tables n., backgammon, 172 [O.F. *table*].

tak v., take, 259 [O.N. *taka*].

take v., p.p. **taka**, 64.

tale n., tale, 770 [O.E. *talu*].

tarie v., delay, keep back, detain, 505 [O.E. *tergan*].

tellen v., tell, disclose, 9 [O.E. *tellan*].

temperaunce n., moderation, restraint, 57 [O.F. *temperance*].

temple n., temple, 662 [O.F. *temple*].

tere n., tear, 166 [O.E. *tēar*].

terme n., technical term, 560 [O.F. *terme*].

than adv., then, than, 66 [O.E. *þonne*].

thanke v., thank, 576 [O.E. *þancian*].

that pron., that, who, 702 [O.E. *þæt*].

then adv., then, at that time, 441 [O.E. *þonne*].

thennes adv., thence, 232 [O.E. *þannes*].

ther adv., there, 51 [O.E. *þĕr*].

ther adv., where, 73 [O.E. *þĕr*].

ther-as adv., where, whither, 486 [O.E. *þĕr + as*].

therby adv., near to it, 387 [O.E. *þĕrbi*].

ther-inne adv., therein, 103 [O.E. *þĕr + inne*].

therto adv., moreover, 7 [O.E. *þĕr + tō*].

ther-with adv., moreover, in addition, 203 [O.E. *þĕr + wiδ*].

thider adv., thither, to that place, 763 [O.E. *þider*].

thilke adj., the same, 160 [O.E. *þylce*].

thing n., thing, possession, 751 [O.E. *þing*].

thinke v., ponder, meditate, 129 [O.E. *þyncan*].

thinketh v., it seems, 670 [O.E. *þynceth*].

thise adj., these, 140 [O.E. *þes*].

tho adv., then, 284 [O.E. *þan*].

thogh conj., although, 591 [O.E. *þoh*].

thoght n., anxiety, thought, 94 [O.E. *þōht*].

thonke v., thank, 817 [O.E. *þancian*].

though conj., though, 826 [O.E. *þēah*].

thoughte v., it seemed, 473 [O.E. *þuhte*].

thral n., servant, slave, 41 [O.E. *þral*].

thretty adj., thirty, 640 [O.E. *þrītig*].

thridde adj., third, 731 [O.E. *þridda*].

thriftily adv., politely, encouragingly, 446 [O.N. *þrifti + līce*].

thurgh prep., by means of, 137 [O.E. *þurh*].

thus adv., thus, in this way, 695 [O.E. *þus*].

til conj., until, 103 [O.N. *til*].

til prep., to, towards, 880 [O.N. *til*].

tiraunt n., tyrant, absolute monarch, 659 [O.F. *tirant*].

to adv., too, 187 [O.E. *tō*].

toke v., p.t. **tak**, 512.

told v., p.t. **tellen**, 737.

Toletanes adj., adapted to Toledo, 545 [O.F. *Toletane*].

to-morwe adv., to-morrow, 505 [O.E. *to-morgen*].

took v., p.t. **tak**, 674.

torment n., torment, suffering, 356 [Lat. *tormentum*].

touche v., reach, touch, 387 [O.F. *toucher*].

touchinge prep., concerning, about, 402 [O.F. *touch + inge*].

toun n., town, city, 673 [O.E. *tūn*].

trappe n., trap, snare, 613 [O.F. *trappe*].

traunce n., trance, 353 [O.F. *transe*].

travaille n., pains, trouble, 889 [O.F. *travaille*].

tregetour n., juggler, magician, conjurer, 413 [O.F. *tresgetteres*].

trespas n., sin, wrong, transgression, 638 [O.F. *trespas*].

tretee n., discussion, 491 [O.F. *traite*].

trewe adj., true, faithful, 30 [O.E. *trēowe*].

trewely adv., truly, indeed, faithfully, 182 [O.E. *trēowe + līce*].

treweste adj., truest, most faithful, 811 [O.E. *trēowest*].

trouthe n., truth, troth, promise, honour, 31 [O.E. *trēwþe*].

turn v., turn away, depart, 283 [O.E. *turnan*].

tusked adj., provided with tusks, 526 [O.E. *tusc + ed*].

tweye adj., two, 567 [O.E. *twegen*].

tweyne adj., two, twain, 334 [O.E. *twegen*].

two adj., two, 663 [O.E. *twa*].

tyme n., time, opportunity, occasion, circumstances, 57 [O.E.*tima*].

tyraunt n., tyrant, 640 [O.F. *tirant*].

unburied adj., unburied, 713 [O.E. *un + buried*].

under prep., under, beneath, within, 381 [O.E. *under*].

undertake v., declare, be certain, 483 [O.E. *under + O.N. taka*].

unnethe adv., scarcely, with difficulty, 8 [O.E. *uneðe*].

unresonable adj., inexplicable, purposeless, 144 [O.F. *un + raisonable*].

un-to prep., towards, to, 237 [O.L.G. *unto*].

untrewe adj., untrue, unfaithful, 256 [O.E. *un + trēowe*].

unwar adj., unwary, 628 [O.E. *un + wær*].

unwiting adj., ignorant, 208 [O.E. *un + witing*].

up prep., upon, 753 [O.E. *up*].

up-on prep., upon, the occasion of, about, 197 [O.N. *uppa*].

use v., practise, 565 [O.F. *user*].

value n., worth, value, 845 [O.F. *value*].

vayn n., uselessness, worthlessness, 244 [Lat. *vanus*].

venquisse v., overcome, put to flight, 46 [O.F. *vaincre*].

verray adj., true, utter, very, 132 [O.F. *verai*].

vertu n., virtue, 45 [O.F. *vertu*].

vertuous adj., pure-minded, capable, 205 [Lat. *virtuosum*].

vileinye n., shameful deed, evil, 676 [O.F. *vilenie*].

virelay n., virelay (see note), 220 [O.F. *virelaie*].

vitaille n., food, 176 [O.F. *vitaille*].

vouche' sauf v., grant, permit, deign, 315 [O.F. *voucher + sauf*].

voyde v., empty, get rid of, 422 [O.F. *voider*].

vyne n., vine, 420 [O.F. *vine*].

waillen v., wail, lament, 620 [O.N. *va*

wake v., lie awake, 91 [O.E. *wacian*].

walk v., walk, 120 [O.N. *valka*].

wan v., p.t. **winne**, 673.

war adj., careful, wary, 813 [O.E. *wær*].

warisshe v., free, cure, 128 [O.F. *garir*].

water n., water, lake, 416 [O.E. *wæter*].

waxen v., grow, become, 517 [O.E. *weaxan*].

way n., way, manner, 689 [O.E. *weg*].

wayle v., wail, weep, lament, 91 [O.N. *veila*].

wayte v., watch for, await, 535 [O.F. *waiter*].

weep v., p.t. **wepe**.

wel adv., truly, assuredly, quite, even, 8 [O.E. *wel*].

welfare n., well-being, condition, 110 [M.L.G. *wolvare*].

welle n., fountain, well, spring, 170 [O.E. *welle*].

wende v., p.t. **wene**, suppose, 613.

wende v., p.t. **wenden**, 895.

wenden v., go, proceed [O.E. *wendan*].

wene v., suppose, 539 [O.E. *wenan*].

went v., p.p. **wenden**, 243.

wente v., p.t. **wenden**, 895.

wepe v., weep, 752 [O.E. *wepan*].

werche v., work, undertake, 5 [O.E. *wyrcan*].

were v., p.t. subj. was, 5.

werk n., work, deed, trouble, 142 [O.E. *weorc*].

werre n., trouble, war, 29 [O.F. *werre*].

wex v., p.t. **waxen**, become, grow, 517.

wey n., way, journey, 441 [O.E. *weg*].

whan conj., when, 71 [O.E. *hwanne*].

whanne conj., when, 678 [O.E. *hwanne*].

what adj., whatever, 264 [O.E. *hwæt*].

what adv., why, 437, 822 [O.E. *hwæt*].

what adv., partly, 509 [O.E. *hwæt*].

wher conj., whether, 570 [O.E. *hwēr*].

wher-as adv., where, 74 [O.E. *hwēr + as*].

wherfore adv., for which reason, 327 [O.E. *hwǣ*

wher-so conj., whether, 50 [O.E. *hwǣ*

whether conj., whether, 358 [O.E. *hwæðer*].

which pron., who, which, whom, 192 [O.E. *hwilc*].

whiderward adv., whither, to what place,
782 [O.E. *hwider* + *weard*].

why adv., why, for what reason, 622 [O.E. *hwī*].

whyl conj., while, 390 [O.E. *hwīles*].

wight n., person, 51 [O.E. *wiht*].

wighte n., weight, 832 [O.E. *wiht*].

wikked adj., wicked, 871 [O.E. *wikke*].

wil n., will, wish, desire, 17 [O.E. *willa*].

willen v., will, wish, intend, 653 [O.E. *willan*].

wind n., wind, 160 [O.E. *wind*].

winne v., win, 348 [O.E. *winnan*].

wirkyng n., calculation, working, 552 [M.H.G. *wirkunge*].

wis adv., certainly, 742 [O.E. *wis*].

wisly adv., wisely, in her wisdom, 61 [O.E. *wīs* + *līce*].

wiste v., p.t. **witen**, 231.

wit n., understanding, intelligence, senses, 147 [O.E. *wit*].

witen v., know, understand, 313.

with prep., with, by means of, 247 [O.E. *wiδ*].

withoute adv., outwardly, 383 [O.E. *wiδūtan*].

withoute(n) prep., without, 721 [O.E. *wiδūtan*].

witnesse n., witness, 639 [O.E. *witness*].

wo n., woe, sorrow, grief, distress, 9 [O.E. *wā*].

woful adj., woeful, sorrowful, wretched, 510 [O.E. *wōful*].

wol v., intend, wish, will, desire, 30 [O.E. *willen*].

wolde v., p.t. **willen**, would, 24.

wolden v., p.t. (plural) **willen**, 653.

wonder adj., wondrous, wonderful, strange, 447 [O.E. *wundor*].

wondren v., wonder, 786 [O.E. *wundrian*].

wonne v., p.p. **winnen**, 5.

woot v., know, p.t. **witen**, 157, 313 [O.E. *witan*].

word n., word, 247 [O.E. *word*].

world n., world, 138 [O.E. *weorold*].

worship n., renown, fame, standing, 83 [O.E. *weorδ* + *scipe*].

worthinesse n., true worth, honour, 10 [O.E. *weorδi* + *nesse*].

worthy adj., distinguished, notable, 59 [O.E. *weorδig*].

wounde n., wound, 688 [O.E. *wund*].

wrappe v., entangle, 628 [Ety. dub.].

wrecche adj., wretched, miserable, 292 [O.E. *wræcc*].

wrecchednesse n., mean action, wickedness, 543 [O.E. *wrechednesse*].

wreke v., avenge, 56 [O.E. *wrecan*].

wreye v., reveal, betray, 216 [O.E. *wrēgan*].

wroghte v., p.t. **werche**, work, perform, 5.

wyde adj., wide, 688 [O.E. *wĭd*].

wyf n., wife, woman, 69 [O.E. *wīf*].

wyfhod n., womanhood, wifeliness, 723 [O.E. *wīfhād*].

wyfly adj., befitting a wife, wifely, 725 [O.E. *wīf* + *lĭc*].

wyke n., week, 567 [O.E. *wice*].

wyn n., wine, 54 [O.E. *wīn*].

wyrche v., work [O.E. *wyrcan*].

wys adj., wise, 63 [O.E. *wys*].

wys adv., certainly, 742 [O.E. *wiss*].

wyse n., manner, fashion, 3 [O.E. *wīse*].

wyve n., wife, 15 [O.E. *wīf*].

yaf v., p.t. **yeve**, 255.

y-cleped v., named, 210 [O.E. *y-cleped*].

ydel n., uselessness, purposelessness, 139 [O.E. *īdel*].

ye adv., certainly, indeed, yes, 744 [O.E. *gēa*].

yě n., eye, 464 [O.E. *ēage*].

yeer n., year, years, 78 [O.E. *gēar*].

yerd n., garden, 523 [O.E. *geard*].

yere n., year, 340 [O.E. *gēar*].

yet adv., still, nevertheless, 262 [O.E. *gĕt*].

yeve v., give, 305 [O.E. *giefan*].

yfostred adj., benefited, 146 [O.E. *fostrian*].

yfounde v., p.p. found, 542.

yfynde v., find, discover, come across, 425 [O.E. *findan*].

yis interj., yes, indeed, 639 [O.E. *gĭse*].

yit adv., yet, 849 [O.E. *gĕt*].

yive v., p.p. **yeve**, 722.

y-knowe v., p.p. **knowe**, 159.

y-laft v., p.p. **leve**, 400.

y-nogh adj., enough, 891 [O.E. *genog*].

yond adv., yonder, over there, 598 [O.E. *geondan*].

yong adj., young, 205 [O.E. *geong*].

yore adv., of long ago, formerly, 235 [O.E. *geare*].

yow pron., you, 603 [O.E. *eow*].

y-payed v., p.p. **paye**, 690.

y-sene v., p.p. **seen**, 268.

y-slayn v., p.p. **sleen**, 637.

y-stiked v., p.p. **stike**, 748.

y-sworn v., p.p. **swerian**, 310.

y-voyded v., p.p. **voyde**, 422.

y-wis adv., indeed, certainly, 635 [O.E. *gewiss*].

Brodie's Notes

D. H. Lawrence	The Rainbow
D. H. Lawrence	Sons and Lovers
D. H. Lawrence	Women in Love
Harper Lee	To Kill a Mockingbird
Laurie Lee	Cider with Rosie
Christopher Marlowe	Dr Faustus
Arthur Miller	The Crucible
Arthur Miller	Death of a Salesman
John Milton	Paradise Lost
Robert C. O'Brien	Z for Zachariah
Sean O'Casey	Juno and the Paycock
George Orwell	Animal Farm
George Orwell	1984
J. B. Priestley	An Inspector Calls
J. D. Salinger	The Catcher in the Rye
William Shakespeare	Antony and Cleopatra
William Shakespeare	As You Like It
William Shakespeare	Hamlet
William Shakespeare	Henry IV Part I
William Shakespeare	Julius Caesar
William Shakespeare	King Lear
William Shakespeare	Macbeth
William Shakespeare	Measure for Measure
William Shakespeare	The Merchant of Venice
William Shakespeare	A Midsummer Night's Dream
William Shakespeare	Much Ado about Nothing
William Shakespeare	Othello
William Shakespeare	Richard II
William Shakespeare	Romeo and Juliet
William Shakespeare	The Tempest
William Shakespeare	Twelfth Night
George Bernard Shaw	Pygmalion
Alan Sillitoe	Selected Fiction
John Steinbeck	Of Mice and Men and The Pearl
Jonathan Swift	Gulliver's Travels
Dylan Thomas	Under Milk Wood
Alice Walker	The Color Purple
W. B. Yeats	Selected Poetry

ENGLISH COURSEWORK BOOKS

Terri Apter	Women and Society
Kevin Dowling	Drama and Poetry
Philip Gooden	Conflict
Philip Gooden	Science Fiction
Margaret K. Gray	Modern Drama
Graham Handley	Modern Poetry
Graham Handley	Prose
Graham Handley	Childhood and Adolescence
R. J. Sims	The Short Story